Rooted and Grounded

Rooted and Grounded

*Faith formation and the
Christian tradition*

Edited by

Steven Croft

CANTERBURY
PRESS
Norwich

© The Contributors 2019

First published in 2019 by the Canterbury Press Norwich
Editorial office
3rd Floor, Invicta House
108–114 Golden Lane
London ECIY OTG, UK
www.canterburypress.co.uk

Canterbury Press is an imprint of Hymns Ancient & Modern Ltd
(a registered charity)

Hymns Ancient & Modern® is a registered trademark of
Hymns Ancient & Modern Ltd
13A Hellesdon Park Road, Norwich,
Norfolk NR6 5DR, UK

British Library Cataloguing in Publication data

A catalogue record for this book is available
from the British Library

978 1 78622 168 1

Typeset by Manila Typesetting
Printed and bound in Great Britain by
CPI Group (UK) Ltd

Contents

Contributors

The Rt Revd Dr Steven Croft is the Bishop of Oxford and formerly the Bishop of Sheffield. He is one of the principal authors of the Pilgrim materials and *The Pilgrim Way*.

The Revd Canon Professor Sarah Foot is Regius Professor of Ecclesiastical History in the University of Oxford and a Canon of Christ Church, Oxford.

The Revd Professor Susan Gillingham is Professor of the Interpretation of the Hebrew Bible in the University of Oxford and Fellow of Worcester College, Oxford.

Canon Professor Carol Harrison is Lady Margaret Professor of Divinity in the faculty of Theology and Religion in the University of Oxford and a Canon of Christ Church, Oxford.

The Revd Canon Dr Simon Jones is Chaplain and Fellow of Merton College, Oxford. He is an Honorary Canon of Christ Church, Oxford, and a Wiccamical Prebendary (Honorary Canon Theologian) of Chichester Cathedral. He is a member of the Church of England Liturgical Commission, and the University of Oxford Faculty of Theology and Religion.

The Revd Professor Alister McGrath is Andreas Idreos Professor of Science and Religion in the University of Oxford, Director of the Ian Ramsey Centre for Science and Religion and a Fellow of Harris Manchester College, Oxford.

The Revd Canon Professor Jennifer Strawbridge is Associate Professor in New Testament at Oxford and Fellow in Theology at Mansfield College. She is a Wiccamical Prebendary (Honorary Canon Theologian) of Chichester Cathedral, an Associate Priest at St Andrew's, Headington, and a member of the Church of England Liturgical and Faith and Order Commissions.

Introduction

A lazy deacon called Deogratias once wrote to his bishop to ask for a sermon he could preach to people enquiring about the Christian faith: here are people who want to know more, who are just at the cusp of wanting to learn about faith and baptism. 'What should I tell them?'

His bishop, Augustine of Hippo (AD 354–430), writes back and offers him a short book: *On Instructing Beginners in the Faith*. It's one of the best books ever written about the cluster of ministries and disciplines the Church calls catechesis. Augustine does supply a sermon – in fact he offers two. But he offers much more.

The most important thing Augustine says about this ministry is this: do it with joy. It is joy that will make the difference.

> Our greatest concern is much more about how to make it possible for those who offer instruction in the faith to do so with joy. For the more they succeed in this, the more appealing they will be. (2.4)

There is no greater joy than walking with young people and with adults as they discover or rediscover faith in Jesus Christ.

But that sets up the question of why has this ministry corporately fallen so far down our priorities? By and large clergy don't feel well equipped in catechesis and nor do lay ministers. We are somewhat de-skilled and our motivation is low. Augustine is also very honest, and he offers Deogratias some reasons for this in his day. They sound very relevant to us today.

We are slow to come to this ministry sometimes because we prefer to study deeper things; we have graduated from the ABC of faith. Perhaps we enjoy other activities in ministry more. Perhaps anxiety or scandal distract us. Perhaps our confidence is low. We have lost our first love and because of our long ministry, because it's so hard, we have become grumpy and disagreeable. Or is it simply that our diary planning is poor? There is always so much to do. This is the one task we want to do but which never comes to the top of the agenda.

As we look back over the long history of the Church, we see that in every period of mission, growth and expansion, the Church has taken this cluster of ministries really seriously. In each period of church history, the development of catechesis in the practices of the Church has been different – there has been much faithful improvisation of the same core principles.

The goal of this collection of essays is not to tell you to approach this ministry in a particular way. The goal is to help us together to work with the Spirit in the renewal of catechesis for our own day.

Seven conversations; six days of prayer and five of study

In Lent 2018, I invited 120 people from across the city of Oxford to come together from every parish and from many of the chaplaincies in seven different conversations around renewing catechesis in our day. We listened and learned together. In early September I set aside six days to walk across the city and visit every parish church and pray for the renewal of these ministries. In November we held five study days for 450 clergy and lay ministers across the Diocese of Oxford.

The listening and conversation informed our prayer together and our prayer informed our study and learning and this is in turn is shaping our practice.

I invited six guest theologians to take a deep dive into one part of scripture or the great tradition of catechesis to resource the Spirit's work of renewal in these ministries. Their talks form the core of this book, together with my opening address. I've been a student of these ministries for over 30 years now. I know something of the depth of insight from the tradition, but I don't know of an accessible guide for ordinands and lay ministers in training or for parish clergy which supports this kind of exploration.

An overview

In the opening chapters I offer an exposition of Luke's story of the Road to Emmaus and four essential elements in catechesis together with a simple overview of the way the Church has engaged in these ministries down the years.

Simon Jones explores the relationship between worship and catechesis in the early Church and today. Carol Harrison looks at the relationship between the work of God's Spirit in forming new Christians and our own partnership in this ministry through the lens of Augustine and Gregory of Nyssa.

The two central essays are biblical. Jennifer Strawbridge explores the key parts of the New Testament which were most used in Christian formation in the early centuries of the Church. Susan Gillingham takes an in-depth look at the Psalter and the ways in which the psalms form us in the faith.

Sarah Foot takes a deep dive into the Anglo-Saxon tradition and explores the remarkable period of English history in which the whole of England heard and responded to the gospel, as described by the Venerable Bede. Alister McGrath offers an overview of the creeds and their importance in Christian formation in every period.

Renewal through scripture and the tradition

The Church is renewed by the grace of God through engaging afresh with scripture and the tradition. We have reached a moment in our long journey when we need again to renew the cluster of ministries of welcome and accompaniment to baptism, of Christian formation, of learning and teaching enquirers. Technology is changing the way the world communicates in radical ways. The questions people ask are different in the twenty-first century. But the core principles of catechesis remain the same. There is much we can learn from earlier generations in our renewal of these ministries in our own day.

How do adults come to faith: A foundation for catechesis

STEVEN CROFT

I too decided, after investigating everything carefully from the very beginning, to write an orderly account for you, most excellent Theophilus, so that you may know the truth concerning the things about which you have been instructed. (Luke 1.3–4)

Luke is a profound theologian of formation. He writes with a particular and explicit purpose: to help his reader, whose name means 'the one who loves God', or 'the one who is God's friend' to know the truth about the things in which he has been, literally, *catechized*. Luke is like the other Gospels: written to nurture and support those who are exploring Christian faith and those who have been baptized and are continuing in the journey.

Luke is fascinated by how people come to faith. He punctuates his great narrative in the Gospel and in his second book, the Acts of the Apostles, with stories that still shape our understanding: the story of the father and the two sons with the account of the younger son travelling away, turning round and coming back (Luke 15.11–32); the parable of the sower with, in Luke's Gospel, a very concise account of what the four kinds of soil mean and the different stages of the germination of a seed and growth of a young plant (8.11–15); the conversion of Saul on the Damascus Road, a paradigm story of conversion told not once nor twice but three times through Acts (9.1–19; 22.6–16 and 26.12–18); the story of

Zacchaeus (Luke 19.1–10); Philip and the Ethiopian eunuch on the road to Gaza (Acts 8.26–40); Peter and the Roman centurion Cornelius (Acts 10.1–48), Lydia opening her heart and home in Philippi (Acts 16.11–15) and many others.

At the very centre of the narrative, at the end of the Gospel and halfway through the arc of the two books read together, Luke sets the longest of his stories of formation: the journey to Emmaus on the day of resurrection.

Luke tells the story of the resurrection in a single day in the final chapter of the Gospel: at the tomb in the early morning (24.1–12); on the road to Emmaus in the middle of the day (24.13–35); in the upper room and then Bethany in the evening (24.36–53). In Luke's theology, of course, Jerusalem is where the disciples are meant to be between Easter and Pentecost. To understand the Emmaus Road we therefore need to know that the two disciples when we meet them are travelling in the wrong direction. Once they have recognized the risen Christ, they are turned around, a literal conversion, and return to the city.

The Emmaus Road is unique among the Easter stories because of the ways in which the disciples recognize the risen Christ. They recognize Christ not suddenly but gradually and not in extraordinary and unrepeatable miracles but through the means of grace which are accessible to the Church in every age: first in fellowship, then in scripture, then in the breaking of the bread, and finally in common witness: the Lord is risen.

In the Emmaus Road, Luke helps us to see more clearly and distinguish four key elements of formation and catechesis. Luke is shining a light through a prism and helping us to see that catechesis is not one element alone. Christian formation is addressed to the whole person. Good, deep, transformative Christian formation embraces each of these four elements and weaves between them in any individual journey to faith. I want to unfold them for us now and then, as it were, put them back together in the faith journeys both of adults and of children. The understanding of catechesis I very much want us to develop together is a catechesis that embraces each and all of them and weaves them into a single whole. In each of them our calling as a Church is to be Christ-like.

Listening and forming community

The first element is being with people in their journey, listening and forming community through the asking of gentle questions.

It is always very sobering to ask the question, where in Luke's Gospel do we first meet the risen Christ on Easter Day. The answer is here, on the road to Emmaus, with the two disciples who are walking in the wrong direction. In Luke's Gospel, we visit the tomb early in the morning but we do not yet see Jesus. The risen Christ, as it were, leaves the 99 and comes in search of the two who are heading in the wrong direction and spends the whole day with them. Jesus is conscious that the Spirit is at work here beyond the community. Jesus is looking for where God is at work and seeking to join in.

The comforting stranger draws near and walks with them. The first time we meet the child Jesus in Luke's Gospel, his parents, frantic with worry, find him in the temple, sitting and listening and asking questions (Luke 2.46). Almost the last time we meet Jesus in Luke we find the mirror of that story: Christ is walking and listening and asking questions. The risen Christ's mode of discourse is not propositional but conversational. 'What are you discussing together as you walk along?' (24.17). They stand still, looking sad. Jesus listens to the pain. Then he asks again, 'What things?', and the story unfolds.

Catechesis builds on gentle pastoral work, being with. Here is our first challenge. For there to be a renewal of catechesis in our Church we must first of all be able to do what the risen Christ does: spend time with people who are going in the wrong direction. We must spend time with people who are outside the Christian community in such a way that we are able to listen, and listen well, to the grief and questions. We need to build a depth of relationship and seek out the places and the people where God is at work.

It is no use rooting ourselves within our churches and communities as the world changes around us and shouting our gospel messages ever more stridently. We must go to where people are and listen to the questions and pain and grief of the world and seek out the agenda of other people by our careful listening. For that to happen we need, as a Church and as individual disciples, to be contemplative (attentive to where God is at work already); compassionate (able to love those who are very different from us) and courageous (willing to ask the hard question, to listen and when the time is right to speak).

Every step in the first part of the journey takes the disciples further away from Jerusalem. There are no quick fixes in formation. We are to fall in step and listen and create community. It is only when trust and welcome have been built that people will be able to listen to what we have to say.

These listening relationships and communities of formation have been built in different ways throughout the history of the Church as we shall see from the catechumenate of the patristic Church, through the monasteries and churches of Anglo-Saxon England, to the parish churches of the Reformation and to the classes and bands of the Methodist revivals. They need to be built in different ways today. But that listening and community will always need to play a role before the way is open for the second element in the Emmaus story: teaching and interpretation from the scriptures.

Interpreting the scriptures

'Then beginning with Moses and all the prophets, he interpreted to them the things concerning himself in all the scriptures' (Luke 24.7). The two disciples encounter the risen Christ in the breaking open of the word. They are to say to each other later in the day: 'Were not our hearts burning within us while he was talking to us on the road, while he was opening the scriptures to us?' (28.32).

4

Formation in all the scriptures plays a key role in effective catechesis in every generation. How should we frame and shape our teaching in the light of this? The first and most obvious point is that our catechesis, the content of our learning and teaching flows not from ourselves but from the scriptures.

Luke's stories use language extremely carefully. In just these few verses we can derive vital principles. Jesus' engagement with the scriptures is first panoramic. The whole story is here from creation to new creation. Jesus' engagement with the scriptures is second Christocentric. Jesus interprets the things concerning himself in all the scriptures. In the same way Jesus Christ is to be at the centre of all of our teaching. Third, Jesus' engagement with the scriptures is interpretation, not simple exposition. We all need help in interpreting and understanding the scriptures. Engagement with the bible of itself does not make strong Christians. We need learn how to read the bible well and interpret the scriptures as the foundation of our catechesis.

If the first stage in the renewal of catechesis is a renewal of our sense of mission – spending time with those who are outside the Church – the second must involve a renewal of our own engagement with scriptures in ways that are panoramic, Christocentric and interpretative. Across the centuries, the great tradition of Christian formation through scripture, the content of our teaching, has focused on a small number of key texts to be learned by heart. There is wisdom in this great tradition.

Two are always present from earliest times and in every generation since. The Apostles' Creed is the key to giving the panoramic view of the story of salvation, as Alister McGrath argues below, and of scripture from creation to new creation and the interpretative keys to the scriptures. Many of the tools for teaching and learning the faith developed over the last thirty years, most notably the Alpha course, have this creedal shape. The Lord's Prayer is the second text universally used to form and shape faith. As we anticipate the next great movement in the Emmaus Road story, formation in faith is not only about learning doctrine but about being drawn into a relationship with God in prayer and sacrament. Cyprian was Bishop of Carthage in the third century. He has passed down to us a series of sermons on the Lord's Prayer in which he expounds the whole gospel through this one text.

At different times in the story of the Church, the most basic catechesis has engaged also with the Commandments as with Luther's catechism and the Prayer Book catechism and at times also the Beatitudes.

The Church of England report *On the Way* in the 1990s began to develop an Anglican understanding of catechesis which continually returns to and is formed by these four great texts. From earliest times, the Church developed simple catechisms in a question and answer format, largely based around these four texts, as a way of teaching the Christian faith to children and young people and adults. The texts and some other material can easily be learned by heart and form the basis for a lifetime's understanding of faith.

Formation in prayer and the sacraments

The third and fourth great movements in the Emmaus Road story I have partly anticipated and will address more briefly.

'As they came near the village to which they were going, he walked ahead as if he were going on' (Luke 24.28). There is something of the gentleness of true Christian catechesis here – making space for the enquirer and for personal response. 'But they urged him strongly saying, "Stay with us, because it is almost evening and the day is now nearly over"' (24.29). There is a strong Lukan irony in that little phrase. For Luke, this is the Day of Resurrection and it will never end.

'So he went in to stay with them. When he was at table with them, he took bread, blessed and broke it and gave it to them. Then their eyes were opened and they recognized him, and he vanished from their sight' (24.29–31).

Later again they will tell each other and the main group of disciples 'how he had been made known to them in the breaking of the bread' (24.35).

Christian formation is not formation in knowledge or understanding of doctrine but in relationship with the risen Christ. Our understanding leads us into friendship with God and love for God. That relationship is expressed in prayer and in the sacraments, the means of grace, both baptism and the Eucharist. A key part of Christian formation is nurturing this relationship and encounter with God in many different ways.

Again, where formation is effective in the Church today, you can see the evidence of quiet days and retreats, Holy Spirit weekends, parish weekends and conferences, visits to New Wine or Walsingham or Soul Survivor where there is an opportunity to meet with God in worship, prayer and sacrament and for that encounter and relationship to deepen and to grow.

Renewal in catechesis again is not simply to add something to the life of the Church. This renewal means continually to deepen and resource that strong spiritual centre to the life of our churches and schools so that there is space for encounter with God in the ordinary and in the special and particular moment.

Formation in Christian mission

Finally, the fourth movement is the return journey from Emmaus to Jerusalem and the bearing witness to this encounter with the risen Christ in the upper room with the disciples and from there in the whole of their lives: 'Then they told what had happened on the road, and how he had been made known to them in the breaking of the bread' (24.35).

This part of the story bears witness to the deep truth that we are formed in our Christian faith through being sent out as well as through being drawn together. When Jesus calls the twelve disciples in Mark 3, they are appointed 'to be with him and to be sent out' (3.14). This is one of the earliest descriptions in the New Testament of what it means to be a disciple and to be the Church, the new Israel, the people of God. In every generation, we are called to live in the dynamic rhythm of drawing near to God's grace in community and fellowship and being sent out to live to God's glory, the rhythm of loving God and loving our neighbour as ourselves.

Sometimes in the life of the Church we fail to understand this dynamic of formation. We imagine that one part of the heartbeat is about learning (coming together to be with Jesus) and the second part is about mission (living our whole lives in love and service out of what we have learned). This is a profound misunderstanding.

We learn and we are formed in both places: we learn new lessons about discipleship and character in the workplace, in the family, in our friendships and in our voluntary service as much as in the life of the Church. If we do not have opportunities to serve and engage in mission through our lives and our churches then we are in danger of becoming consumer Christians and we will not learn and grow.

John and Charles Wesley and their colleagues made a significant contribution to reimagining catechesis in their generation. They rediscovered the importance of moving outside the church in listening and community and telling the story of the good news as Wesley began to preach to the miners in Bristol in the open air. There were many powerful instances of conversion. But the movement grew and deepened because Wesley built places of formation and catechesis in the bands and the class system. These were places where above all the new Christians learned to live out their faith in everyday life through giving an account to one another and through reflection on scripture in the light of everyday discipleship.

Renewing catechesis

What do we learn from the risen Christ on the Emmaus Road?

Renewal in catechesis is not about the implementation of a programme. Indeed I do not have a programme for you to implement, nor do any of the authors who have contributed to this book. The renewal of catechesis is about the renewal of the time we spend outside the Christian community, listening and asking gentle questions and forming community. It is about the renewal of our understanding of the scriptures and our ability to teach them in depth to those who are enquirers and new Christians so as to lay a broad and deep foundation. It is about the renewal of our life of prayer and sacrament and enabling moments of significant encounter with the risen Christ. It is about deepening our common commitment to everyone so that all can live out the Christian faith through communities of mutual support.

As you begin to engage with the material in this book, I would invite you to spend a few minutes in reflection on the ways in which these different elements have played their part in your own journey of faith and in the stories of those you know well. It may be that you would emphasize one more than the other, but see if you can reflect on your own journey and the mystery of God's work in you differently in the light of this story.

It seems to me that as adults come to faith these four elements of catechesis will often play a part over a timespan of several years, not always in the same order. Something awakens a search for faith. That search and openness to enquiry is met with gentle listening and friendship which evokes an honest questioning. There will often be an opportunity to talk about painful experiences in life and sometimes the chance to form new communities with others on a similar journey.

This gentle listening in turn leads to an openness to learning from the scriptures in ways that are panoramic and tell the whole story of salvation, and in ways that set Christ at the centre of our learning. The key texts of the Apostles' Creed and the Lord's Prayer continue to be excellent paths to this careful listening to the scriptures.

Alongside this learning from the scriptures there will be encounters with God in prayer and sacrament. Sometimes (as with Saul on the Damascus Road) these precede any contact with the Christian community. Sometimes they happen as part of and alongside a group formed for catechesis. Sometimes they coincide with a public affirmation of faith and baptism, confirmation and first communion.

And alongside all of this will be a growing desire to be changed and to live differently, a vocation to serve in various ways which again evokes a need for deeper learning, community and support.

For a child or young person, all of these elements need to be present through their experience of church and school: being held in friendship and community; opportunities to learn the faith in different ways according to the scriptures; opportunities for prayer and worship and encounter and a growing understanding of what it means to live out our faith in the whole of our lives.

As parish churches, chaplaincies and schools we are called to provide these four elements of catechesis for adults, for children and for young people, not through special events but through the normal everyday life together and the natural rhythm of the Christian year. Renewing catechesis is about restoring these simple disciplines to the life of our churches, restoring confidence in the life-changing power of the gospel and rebuilding our churches as places of nurture and Christian growth.

2

A very short history of catechesis

STEVEN CROFT

The Church has been welcoming people to baptism and Christian faith for 2000 years. Over that time, as you would expect, some elements and principles have remained constant. Some have changed and evolved according to place and time and culture and with different patterns of communication.

As the essays in this volume demonstrate, there is much that we can learn from the practice of the Church in different places and in earlier generations. We have a rich seam to mine. But that seam is not always very accessible to the student or general reader. The purpose of this chapter is to offer an introduction to some of this history to whet the appetite for further exploration and to shed light on present practice.

The New Testament

The term 'catechesis' is used from the New Testament onwards as a term for Christian formation and preparation for baptism and lifelong discipleship. The term is used for the period of formation beginning from the first enquiry through to and beyond baptism and being established in the faith.

The Gospels were written as tools for catechesis. As we have seen, Luke is explicitly writing to Theophilus 'so that you may know the truth concerning the things about which you have been *catechized*'. John's Gospel begins with the journey of enquirers to Jesus and ends with an appeal to faith:

But these things are written so that you may come to believe that Jesus is the Messiah, the Son of God and, believing, may have life in his name. (John 20.31)

The very heart of catechesis is introducing people to Jesus. The Acts of the Apostles describes the (sometimes idealized) patterns by which people were introduced to Christian faith. In the early Church in Jerusalem there was a pattern of daily formation after baptism:

They devoted themselves to the apostles' teaching and fellowship, to the breaking of bread and the prayers. (Acts 2.42)

Ananias welcomes Saul and offers individual preparation for baptism in Acts 9 involving prayer and the laying on of hands. In Acts 14, Barnabas and Paul revisit the churches they had founded on their first missionary journey and give us some hints of the challenges the new Christians will meet: 'It is through many persecutions that we must enter the kingdom of God.' Suffering is at the heart of the syllabus here. In Acts 19, we have a fascinating glimpse into an early catechumenate in Ephesus as Paul teaches daily in the lecture hall of Tyrannus over several years.

Catechesis is concerned with the whole of Christian formation not simply the learning of facts or doctrine. The Holy Spirit works powerfully within those coming to faith and those who are working with them to support formation and the transformation of life. The focus of formation is being in Christ and like Christ. There is considerable stress on learning patterns of prayer and, as Susan Gillingham argues here, praying in and through the psalms is central to those patterns.

As we have seen, one way of reading the story of the Emmaus road is as a paradigm story of catechesis: Jesus walks with those who are going in the wrong direction away from Jerusalem. The four means Jesus deploys in Christian formation are the building of community through listening; attending to the scriptures; prayer and the sacraments; and engaging in witness and mission. These are four means the Church has used in every age to grow disciples. Together they form the ways in which we discern the risen Christ.

There are four great metaphors for this process of formation in scripture. The first is the journey seen in Exodus and exile; in the story of the two sons; in the Emmaus and Damascus Roads and the earliest description of the Christian faith as the Way.

The other three metaphors are all found in 1 Corinthians 3: Christian formation is a labour of love, like parenting, giving a special diet to those not yet mature; it is a work of partnership with God and with others, like farming, sowing, watering and waiting; it is a work of development, like building, first laying a foundation and then teaching the new disciples how to build well in their own lives.

The word 'catechesis' has at its centre the term 'echo'. Good Christian formation is founded on repetition of certain texts and phrases which become embedded in the heart and become a means of transformation.[1] The aim of Christian formation is to create a resounding inner echo of God's living Word, an image of Christ at the centre of each disciple's life often through learning very simple core texts by heart.

The early Church

Catechesis in the early centuries of the Church was the work of several years of formation and instruction. To be baptized into a Christian minority was a serious decision in an age of intermittent persecution and hostility to Christians.

Catechesis was important and continuous. It shaped much of the ordinary life of the Church, including its worship, as Simon Jones demonstrates. Some parts of the early Church deploy an annual cycle of formation leading up to baptism at Easter. Those who were catechumens and receiving instruction would enrol for baptism in Epiphany, often in response to preaching on particular Sundays.

They would then receive further instruction during the forty days before Easter: the origin of Lent. The rest of the

Church would keep Lent with them as a reminder of their own baptism.[2]

Formation would include community, listening to the scriptures, prayer leading to the sacrament of baptism and the Eucharist at Easter and sharing in God's mission.

Jennifer Strawbridge draws our attention to some of the key passages in Paul's epistles which form a vital part of this early tradition of formation. Eventually, the core texts for instruction were the Apostles' Creed and the Lord's Prayer although a wide variety of scriptures were used.

This pattern of formation was normally led by the bishop and was given priority in his ministry. He was assisted in this by the presbyters and deacons. As Simon demonstrates the period of formation flows into and from powerful and dramatic services of baptism.

This pattern of formation was remarkably effective and led to the sustained growth of the Church, by the grace of God, as a minority community across the Roman empire even despite opposition.

The monastic movements and the medieval Church

From the conversion of Constantine onwards, the Church grew rapidly and became the majority religion of the Empire. Baptism as an infant became the norm, decreasing the focus on adult catechesis as the means of entering the Church.

Much of the wisdom on Christian formation was nurtured and developed thereafter by the monastic movements. The monastery was the place to be supported in living a counter-cultural Christian life in a rhythm of prayer, rest and work. Benedict seeks to establish in his rule 'a school for the Lord's service in which there is nothing sharp and nothing heavy' – an excellent guide in Christian formation.

The deep Christian formation found in the monastery then inspires the work of preaching, teaching and catechesis in local churches. As Sarah Foot demonstrates, Europe was evangelized by religious communities establishing deep places of formation and prayer from which women and men were sent to love and teach the faith.

This pattern is evident in the evangelization of Britain from Ireland from the north and by Augustine of Canterbury from the south. It is evident in the sending of missionaries from Britain into Scandinavia and Germany and in the revival of the great monasteries of France which led eventually to the founding of the great universities.

England 1287–1530

Faith needs to be modelled, lived, taught and retaught in every generation because, in Tertullian's words, Christians are not born but made. The Church continues to reflect on patterns of catechesis that are appropriate locally and nationally.

In the first chapter of his seminal book, *The Stripping of the Altars*, Eamon Duffy describes catechesis in the two centuries before the invention of printing and the English Reformation. In 1281 the Archbishop of Canterbury and the English bishops agreed a Lambeth declaration. The clergy were to expound the Christian faith in every parish no less than four times each year. The content of the faith they were to expound was as follows:

- The Apostles' Creed.
- The seven petitions of the Lord's Prayer.
- The Commandments.
- The seven works of mercy (based on Matthew 25).
- The seven vices.
- The seven virtues.
- The seven sacraments.

These elements formed the basis for the teaching of Christian faith in a largely non-literate and non-book culture before the Reformation.[3] The tradition of the seven vices survives to this day in popular culture as the seven deadly sins.

England 1530–1740

The English Reformers faced a new challenge: the teaching of the recast and reshaped Anglican faith and identity to a population learning to read in the midst of a technological and political revolution.

The key was the development of a simple catechism issued with the *Book of Common Prayer* in 1548 and revised in 1604 and again in 1662.

The catechism is based on Martin Luther's shorter catechism. It is in a simple question and answer format making it easy to learn and remember. It is based around:

- The Apostles' Creed.
- The Lord's Prayer.
- The Ten Commandments.

The catechism was printed as a primer to help people learn to read. People would learn their letters first and then be introduced to their first text: the catechism. This primer became the bestselling book of the sixteenth century in Britain (by far).

The same texts were used in Morning and Evening Prayer and the service of Holy Communion. They were often written on large boards at the front of churches, which can be seen to this day.

All clergy were expected to give instruction in the catechism every Sunday by law, normally before evensong. This pattern persisted over many centuries and was exported across the world. In 2016 I made my first visit to the Diocese of Oxford's link diocese of Kimberley and Kuruman in South Africa. I had some time in the Cathedral on the final Sunday of the visit and noticed in a side chapel a group of teenagers gathered together. They were studying the Trinity as part of their preparation for confirmation in the coming weeks.

As Alister McGrath argues, the Apostles' Creed offers a map for understanding the Christian life. The traditional theological syllabus in the ancient English universities preparing clergy for ministry was designed to equip them for this task of Christian formation – to understand and teach the scriptures and the creeds.

This investment in catechesis by the clergy was pursued with great energy. The *Prayer Book* catechism continued to develop with the familiar words on the sacraments added in 1604. Between 1530 and 1740 there is evidence of over 1,000 different printed catechisms in English. All or part of over 600 still survive.[4]

For clergy, the normal pattern of ministry after ordination and on coming to a new living was first to pay attention to writing and giving the catechetical sermons which were continually revised and renewed throughout a lifetime of ministry.

This focus on catechetical work also results in the *Westminster Shorter Catechism* of 1646 and the powerful series of addresses on catechesis by Richard Baxter, Vicar of Kidderminster, *The Reformed Pastor*, published in 1657 and hugely influential. Both reflect the strong theological currents at work in the Church in England in the seventeenth century.

Catechisms become in this period a way of more closely defining doctrine as this became contested rather than simply a means of teaching and communicating faith. For this reason they became longer and, paradoxically, less useful for teaching enquirers.

The Methodist revivals

John and Charles Wesley and the Methodist movement made a very substantial contribution to the English tradition of catechesis through the creation of special provision for adults who were seeking to learn the faith through bands and classes. John Wesley returned to the principles of the early Church by attending to what was happening outside the churches and preaching to the miners in Bristol. Many thousands came to faith in Christ.

The Wesleys return to the principles of the early Church in setting catechesis at the heart of the life of the local church with remarkable effect not only in Britain but across the world.

There is some evidence that these were imitated in home meetings in Anglican churches through the eighteenth and nineteenth centuries, which also saw the rise of the Sunday School movement and an immense investment in the teaching of the faith to children and young people.

The twentieth century

The disciplined practice of catechesis was in decline and neglected for much of the twentieth century. There are many reasons for the decline of the Church of England during this time but one of the most significant is the neglect of the regular, systematic teaching of the Christian faith to enquirers and new Christians.

The Roman Catholic Church invested significantly in catechesis in the period following the Second Vatican Council, publishing the Rite for the Christian Initiation of Adults in 1974 and the Catechism in 1994.

In the late 1980s and through the 1990s there was something of a revival of catechesis in the Church of England and elsewhere through the development of nurture groups and process evangelism courses (such as Alpha, Emmaus and Christianity Explored). This revival of catechesis remains the principal factor behind the growth in some parts of the Church of England over the last 30 years.

This rediscovery of catechesis was practice led: parishes discovered through trial and error what was effective in nurturing new Christians and then spread that good practice. In the post-war years, Billy Graham and other evangelists preached to call people who had learned the Christian story in childhood back to a living faith. With each decade of the twentieth century, this residual knowledge of the Christian story fell lower and lower. People were beginning further back as adults and needed a much simpler, but deep, introduction to finding faith.

This emerging practice was supported by research (particularly by John Finney and Robert Warren). Theological connections began to be made with the catechetical practice of the early Church and with the Roman Catholic renewal of catechesis.

The Church of England sought to draw its parishes back to the principles of catechesis in the important 1995 report, *On the Way*, and to draw together liturgical practice and Christian formation. *On the Way* argues for a return to four texts at the heart of our learning: the Apostles' Creed, the Lord's Prayer, the Commandments and the Beatitudes. The report was not widely taken up in parishes but remains a key text for the study of the discipline. It had significant influence on the development of the Common Worship initiation services.

In 2012, the House of Bishops of the Church of England commissioned further work on catechesis in what became the Pilgrim course. In developing the Pilgrim materials the four authors (Robert Atwell, Stephen Cottrell, Paula Gooder and myself) sought to work within this long tradition of catechesis by focusing on these four texts and also returning to the Emmaus Road disciplines of listening to create community, attending to scripture, prayer and the sacraments and engaging in mission. Many other bishops and teachers contributed to the development of Pilgrim. Pilgrim has been widely used across the Church since publication.

The Pilgrim Way – a new catechism

The Pilgrim authors printed the (largely forgotten) Revised Catechism of the Church of England as part of the *Pilgrim Leader's Guide*, partly to show we were working in this ancient and modern tradition of catechesis.[5]

In 2015 we began work on a new catechism for Pilgrim, to support new Christians in their journey of faith. *The Pilgrim Way*, a guide to the Christian faith, was published in 2017 and is now at the heart of the faith section of the Church of England website. A range of other resources support its use, including short daily reflections on the four texts available in digital form and as short booklets.

A vital, serious and ever-changing discipline

The story of catechesis is not something that can be learned in an afternoon. It is a serious discipline, vital to the life and health of the Church in every generation. The chapters that follow each explore a different part of this long story.

Notes

1 Carol Harrison, *Listening in the Early Church* (Oxford: Oxford University Press, 2013).

2 See William Harmless, *Augustine and the Catechumenate* (Glendale, AZ: Pueblo, 1995).

3 See Eamon Duffy, *The Stripping of the Altars* (New Haven, CT: Yale University Press, 1992), particularly Ch. 1, 'How Piers the Plowman learned his Paternoster'.

4 See Ian Green, *The Christian's ABC, Catechisms and Catechizing in England, 1530–1740* (New York: Clarendon Press, 1996).

5 See also www.pilgrimcourse.org.

3

Worship transforming catechesis: Catechesis transforming worship

SIMON JONES

A silo mentality is as much a danger to the life of the Church as it is to the life of any workplace, not least when it concerns the relationship between catechesis and worship.

The genius of the catechumenate approach to evangelism is that it combines teaching and worship in an accompanied process of Christian formation. And yet it's sometimes the case that the Church of England shies away from this integrated approach, preferring to put worship and catechesis in their own separate boxes, as being the responsibility of, and intended for, different groups of people. Worship is what the Christian community does when it gathers, and so is for those on the inside of the church building; whereas catechesis is the process of instruction by which people become members of that community, and is for those on the outside, and therefore missional.

Such a dichotomy between catechesis and worship is false and has the potential to undermine the Church's mission. Drawing inspiration and insight from what is known about the history of catechesis in the first four centuries of the Church's history, this chapter will explore three areas and discuss their implications for the Church's mission and ministry:

1 that worship is an essential part of catechesis
2 that catechesis doesn't end once someone is baptized and admitted to communion
3 that all worship is catechetical.

Although it would be easy to dismiss these as pedantic points of liturgical interest, to my mind they are fundamental principles for the Church to grapple with if it's serious about breaking out of the silo mentality that separates catechesis and worship, and unlocking their combined potential as tools for mission.

Catechesis in the early Church

Some of the earliest evidence for the catechumenate comes from the Christian convert, Tertullian, writing in North Africa at the end of the second century. It's Tertullian who famously said that 'Christians are made, not born' and, for Tertullian, this process for making Christians included a period of catechesis followed by a more intensive preparation immediately before the candidate was baptized and admitted to communion. It's not certain how long the period of catechesis lasted, but Tertullian makes clear the liturgical context of the final preparation in one of his treatises on baptism:

> Those who are at the point of entering upon baptism ought to pray, with frequent prayers, fastings, bendings of the knee, and all-night vigils, along with the confession of all their sins, so as to make a copy of the baptism of John.[1]

Moving forward in time, it used to be the case that liturgical scholars would next turn to the *Apostolic Tradition* attributed to Hippolytus as describing Christian worship in Rome in the early third century. Now, however, there is considerable doubt over the document's authorship, date and place of composition. That said, although *Apostolic Tradition* may be a composite work drawing on various liturgical practices from diverse Christian communities, what is says about the catechumenate is still of interest to us, even though we have to be aware that some of what it describes may reflect later, oriental practices rather than third-century western ones.

The first stage in the catechumenal process seems to have involved a potential catechumen being brought by a sponsor, perhaps most likely a friend, to a Christian teacher before one of the regular weekday gatherings for catechesis. The teacher would question the person about why they wanted to become a Christian, what their current situation was, their occupation and way of life. Some professions, such as astrologers and charioteers, were forbidden, and had to be renounced before someone could be admitted into the catechumenate.

Once admitted, *Apostolic Tradition* suggests that the catechumenate lasted for three years, though some people might be fast-tracked depending on their progress. This process involved the catechumens 'hearing the word' in the early morning several times a week, alongside members of the Christian community, and being instructed on what they had heard. The content of the teaching is unclear, but what we are told is that, after the teacher had finished, the two groups, believers and catechumens, separated. The Christian community prayed together and shared the kiss of peace in one place, while the catechumens prayed separately from them without sharing the peace, after which the teacher laid his hands on them, prayed for them and dismissed them so that they could go to their daily work.

At an appropriate time, candidates for baptism were chosen. Here again their way of life was examined: had they visited the sick? Had they done every kind of good work? If their sponsors testified that they had, the catechumenate became more intensive, with daily meetings including further hand layings and exorcisms alongside the instruction. At this point they were able to 'hear the gospel'.

What can be concluded from this? Although the evidence from this period is rather limited, it nevertheless seems clear that prayer, as well as exorcism, was an integral part of catechesis. Of equal significance is the Church's interest in the candidate's way of life, the way in which their Christian character was being formed, which had more to do with learning how to live as a Christian than what to believe. Certainly, in relation to the Church choosing candidates for baptism, being on the way to being formed as a Christian disciple seems to be of greater significance than knowledge of Christian doctrine, but the two are obviously connected, and it would be a mistake to push the distinction too far. As to what *Apostolic Tradition* means when it says that, having been chosen, the catechumens are to 'hear the gospel', it's not at all clear, but it may be that this is when teaching in the credal aspects of Christian doctrine begins.

The separation between the worshipping Christian community and the catechumens is also noteworthy. The latter do not pray with the baptized, they do not share the kiss of peace with them, nor would they observe them celebrating the Eucharist. This is a point to which this chapter will return but, for now, it's worth noting that part of the reason for this, indeed, part of the reason for the delay in doctrinal teaching, if this is what is going on, is the context of persecution in this period before the conversion of Constantine and the Edict of Toleration in 313. Becoming a catechumen was a dangerous business. It involved considerable risk for the candidate, but also for the Church, if someone with malicious intent was admitted. Hence the reason in this period for the *disciplina arcani* (the discipline of the secret), whereby aspects of Christian faith and practice were kept secret from non-Christians and catechumens for fear that knowledge of them would be used as ammunition for persecution.

Catechesis in the fourth century

Moving on to the fourth century, it's hard to over-emphasize the significance of the conversion of Constantine for Christian faith and practice – although 'conversion' is a slightly problematic word in this context, as Constantine only became a catechumen towards the end of his life, and was eventually baptized shortly before his death, so we're probably on safer ground referring to the significance of the Edict of Toleration.

It's not an entirely comfortable story to tell. The fourth century witnesses to a huge increase in numbers of adult and, within a hundred years, infant candidates for baptism. Yet, confronted with this changed and more comfortable reality, the religion of the Empire engages with these larger numbers with a much less rigorous scrutiny about the candidates' motive for baptism and way of life than had previously been the case. As the bar is lowered and becomes easier to jump over, admission to the catechumenate becomes much more part of what the Church does, its bread and butter, ordinary routine. And for those who are admitted, Constantine's example of not rushing to the font becomes the practice of many.

Alan Kreider describes the catechumenate in this period as follows:

> most fourth-century catechumens were not being catechized, except in the most general sense that they were able to go to sermons if they wished. Instead, they were the large, amorphous group of unbaptized 'Christians' hesitating and temporizing, deferring the time when they would be willing to submit themselves to the rigors of conversion.[2]

The situation in which the fourth-century Church found itself has some interesting parallels with twenty-first-century Britain. Although the present-day Church is obviously not emerging from a period of persecution, nevertheless, in many of the contexts in which it ministers it encounters a decreasing number of those who identify as Christian but who don't practise their faith alongside an increasing number of those who identify as spiritual but not religious; as well, of course, as other groups.

If the Church wishes to focus its catechesis on non-practising Christians and the spiritual but not religious, it may be instructive to see how the fourth-century Church responded to its evolving situation. The focus here is on two things: preaching and worship.

In terms of preaching, the fourth century is sometimes referred to as the Golden Age of catechesis. If this is in any way true of this period, it is most obviously so in relation to catechetical writing which, at this time, becomes its own literary genre. The great names here are Cyril of Jerusalem, John Chrysostom, Theodore of Mopsuestia and Ambrose of Milan. If the duration of the catechumenate was ever anything approaching three years, as *Apostolic Tradition* suggests, it is not so now: 40 days in Alexandria, 30 days in Antioch and, in Jerusalem, it most likely took place during the weeks of Lent.

Another important feature is that the instruction is divided into two parts – that which took place before baptism – *catechesis* – and that which took place afterwards – *mystagogy*. Although this teaching is most commonly referred to as being delivered in the form of lectures – catechetical and mystagogical lectures – it's important not to lose sight of the fact that, just as in the earlier period, these lectures were only part of the process of catechesis. Once again, the other chief ingredient was worship and, in the Constantinian period, the way in which rites of initiation were adapted to suit the situation in which the Church now found itself. In short, they were celebrated with a much-heightened sense of drama with some elements from pagan mystery religions, such as the giving of a lighted candle, being introduced with an explicitly Christian, biblical interpretation.

It's very easy to dismiss this as the Church's desperate attempt to make its worship more exciting, more akin to rival ritual forms, to bring upon the candidate a powerful emotional experience that previous generations of Christians might have experienced at a prior moment of conversion. There may be some truth in that position, but it's by no means the whole story. First and foremost, this transformation of the Church's worship in the fourth century is a result both of the intimate relationship that existed between catechesis and worship within the process of conversion, and the Church's confidence in its worship, specifically here its rites of initiation, enabling the candidate to participate in nothing less than the drama of salvation.

Cyril of Jerusalem puts it in this way in one of his mystagogical lectures to the newly baptized:

What a strange and astonishing situation! We did not really die, we were not really buried, we did not really hang from a cross and rise again. Our imitation was symbolic, but our salvation a reality.[3]

Such a theology of worship is evident in the *Apostolic Tradition* where, after the period of instruction, Christians and catechumens go their separate ways, and do not pray together or share the peace. This says as much about a confident sense of these liturgical elements expressing in a profound way the Christian community's communion with Christ and one another as it does about their need to keep certain aspects of liturgical practice secret for fear of persecution.

The West Syrian Theodore of Mopsuestia, writing near Antioch at the end of the fourth century, points to the significance of the peace for his community in this passage from his fourth baptismal homily:

> This kiss which all present exchange constitutes a kind of profession of the unity and charity that exists among them. Each of us gives the kiss of peace to the person next to him, and so in effect gives it to the whole assembly, because this act is an acknowledgment that we have all become the single body of Christ our Lord, and so must preserve with one another that harmony that exists among the limbs of a body, loving one another equally, supporting and helping one another, regarding the individual's needs as concerns of the community, sympathising with one another's sorrows and sharing in one another's joys.[4]

This is, therefore, no empty gesture. It is a dramatic act with profound implications for the identity of the community and the way in which its members are called to relate to one another.

A further aspect of this transformed celebration of catechesis and initiation in the fourth century is the separation between catechetical and mystagogical lectures sandwiching the sacramental celebration. With the exception of Theodore, none of the other great catechists of this period prepare the candidates for what will happen in the dramatic rites of initiation they are about to experience. They can, in a Church that is free to practise its faith, but they choose not to. And that choice comes from confidence in the symbolic power of the liturgy, confidence not only that it points to a reality beyond itself, but also that the use of its symbols (water, oil, light, and so on) bring about what they signify. Cyril explains this to the newly baptized in these words:

> You made the confession that brings salvation, and sub-merged yourselves three times in the water and emerged: by this symbolic gesture you were secretly re-enacting the burial of Christ three days in the tomb . . . In one and the same action we died and were born; the water of salvation became both tomb and mother for you . . . A single moment achieves both ends, and your begetting was simultaneous with your death.[5]

It's hardly surprising, then, that the rites themselves are described by Chrysostom as 'awesome', 'about which it is forbidden to speak';[6] and therefore the explanation of what happens comes not before they are celebrated but afterwards, in the mystagogy, which often includes a challenge for future discipleship. A powerful example of this can be found in a sermon of Ambrose of Milan in which he's talking about the post-baptismal anointing:

> So you were immersed, and you came to the priest. What did he say to you? *God the Father Almighty*, he said, *who has brought you to a new birth through water and the Holy Spirit and has forgiven your sins, himself anoints you into eternal life.* See where the anointing has brought you: 'to eternal life', he says. Do not prefer this present life to eternal life. For example, if an enemy should come against you, wishing to rob you of your faith, if he threatens you with death to make you go astray, consider what choice you should make. Do not choose the life in which you have not been anointed.

Choose the one in which you have been anointed. Choose eternal life rather than this life.[7]

In order to understand what was going on in these fourth-century initiation rites, it is necessary to see the whole process of Christian catechesis and initiation as drama, a drama in several acts. Not that the catechists and clergy are the actors and the catechumens passive spectators, but all are active participants in this drama, which is the drama of salvation.

In the catechetical lectures, the candidates were being taught about the Apostles' Creed, the Lord's Prayer, and they needed to learn those lines so that they could repeat them for themselves before their baptism. But more importantly, through this process that involved prayer, fasting and exorcism, their Christian character was being formed, as it was in the mystagogy that followed their baptism. And so when we talk about catechesis in this period, it's important to see it terms of Christian formation, a dramatic process that involves the whole person and their incorporation into the life of Christ and of his Church.

This brief canter through some elements of catechesis in the first four centuries of the Church's history has revealed that worship is an essential part of catechesis. We've encountered mystagogy, whose existence suggests that the process of catechesis doesn't stop after baptism and admission to communion. And we've seen that, if to worship is to participate in the drama of salvation, then it is to be placed in a crucible in which, with our sisters and brothers in the faith, we are constantly and continuously being formed into the likeness of Christ. All worship is, therefore, catechetical.

Implications for catechesis and worship in the contemporary Church

Before considering some specific implications of this, it will prove helpful to look briefly at the extent to which the contemporary Church of England can be said to have confidence in its worship.

It is a cause for concern that the Church of England doesn't always appear to be particularly bothered about worship. Although the first of the current Archbishop of Canterbury's priorities is the renewal of prayer and the religious life, and worship is found at the top of the mission statements of many dioceses and parishes, the reality is often very different. Part of the reason for this may be the silo mentality, mentioned at the beginning of this chapter, which prioritizes other things above worship because it fails to see that worship is a fundamental part of every aspect of the Church's life. We should not be ashamed to say that the worship of God is the Church's primary vocation, just as it is humanity's primary vocation.

Earlier a parallel was drawn between how Alan Kreider describes the great amorphous mass of catechumens in the fourth century and the Church's contemporary context. It is often said that we're living at a time where there is a renewed sense of interest in worship, not least by those who would describe themselves as Christian, whether or not they've been baptized, but who don't actively practise their faith, and those who would consider themselves as 'spiritual' rather than 'religious'. This presents the Church with an opportunity to revitalize the relationship between worship and catechesis. And yet, across all traditions, this is often hampered by a very noticeable lack of confidence in worship.

Unlike Cyril, Chrysostom, Theodore and Ambrose, the contemporary Church can very easily fall into the trap of *not* believing that worship does what it says on the tin. Remember Cyril's words: 'Our imitation was symbolic, but our salvation a reality.' Do we believe that when we preside at worship we are seeking to lead people into the mystery of God? Do we believe that when scripture is proclaimed, it is the word of God himself speaking to his people, calling them into relationship with himself? Do we believe that when we celebrate the Eucharist together, we are present at the transformation of the world? Do we believe that when we baptize, we are proclaiming the indelible identity of a child of God who, in the waters of the font, experiences an intense life-transforming encounter with Christ crucified and risen through the anointing of the Holy Spirit?

The loss of confidence in worship, which results in worship not proclaiming the reality of salvation, can manifest itself in different ways. For some, worship can easily become entertainment, with the leader's focus shifting from God to the congregation and, from a worthy desire to be inclusive and welcoming, nothing happening without it first being introduced and explained. For others, there is the danger of an inward-looking rubricism, which sees doing it by the book as a primary concern rather than seeing ritual as means of enabling active participation in worship through which people are drawn into the mystery of God. Worship becoming an arena for the practice of priest-craft is as much a danger as worship becoming a stage for entertainment.

To help the Church recognize again that all worship has the potential to be catechetical, and that worship can transform catechesis, and catechesis transform worship, there are some lessons that can be learnt from the fourth century about worship as the drama of salvation. It's worth emphasizing again that we're not talking about actors on a stage and passive spectators in an audience. Authentic worship is a drama in which everyone present is invited to be an active participant – some of them exercising particular roles, but all of them invited to be actively involved in the drama that celebrates the transforming presence of Christ in word, sacrament and the community of the baptized.

If the Church is open to the possibility of seeing catechetical worship as drama, the drama of salvation, in which those who actively participate are formed by a transformative encounter with Christ crucified and risen, the question that follows is what implications does that have for the way in which we plan and lead our worship?

A good starting point is to consider afresh how the celebration of Christian initiation, including the catechumenate Rites on the Way, relates to the worship of the Christian community. *Common Worship* states that baptism is:

much more than a beginning to the Christian life. It expresses the identity which is ours in Jesus Christ and the shape of the life to which we are called . . . Baptism is a reality whose meaning has to be discovered at each stage of a person's life . . . One test of the liturgical celebration of baptism is whether, over time, it enables the whole Church to see itself as a baptized community, called to partake of the life of God and to share in the mission of God to the world.[8]

As a church, we will struggle to reimagine the potential of catechesis if we fail to see ourselves as a baptized and baptizing community.

In the case of infants, research carried out by Sandra Millar as part of the Baptism Project suggests that that there are significant missional advantages to baptizing 'when the most number of people come together' (as the Canons encourage) rather than at a stand-alone service, with those who have their child baptized at a principal Sunday service being more likely to attend church in the future than those who do not.[9]

In the case of adult candidates, if the Church is serious about accompanying them along their journey of faith, it's important that their presence in the worshipping community is highlighted appropriately at different stages. In terms of the drama of the liturgy, they shouldn't be left waiting in the wings until the day of their baptism. The creative use of some of the *Common Worship* Rites on the Way can enable this to happen, and also remind the local community of their own baptismal identity as well as providing an opportunity for them to express their support for the candidates.

A second point that can be taken from the fourth century relates to what has already been said about recovering confidence in worship doing what it says on the tin. To do this, liturgy needs to be given sufficient space to let it speak for itself. This has relevance across different traditions and styles of worship and relates to both texts and symbolism.

In relation to texts, there are three aspects of their use that can potentially suffocate the liturgy: the number of them, our choice of them, and the way in which worshippers encounter them. 'Words, words, words, poor little talkative Christianity', says Mrs Moore in E. M. Forster's *A Passage to India*. Anglican worship can be very wordy. In the Prayer Books of 1549 and 1552 Cranmer replaces much of the ritual of the medieval rites with lengthy exhortations. Within the library of *Common Worship* resources, the Church of England has provided many words for use in worship. The question for us is how we use them responsibly and creatively to enable those whom we seek to serve, enquirers as well as members of the community of faith, to grow spiritually.

In order to give the liturgy space to breathe, 'less is more' is a good principle to follow, with the appropriate use of silence, where that's possible. To do that effectively and to preside confidently, it's necessary to have a clear understanding of what's mandatory and what's optional within each rite and why, how texts and ritual elements relate to each other, and what their purpose is.

The same principle applies when it comes to the choice of texts. Variety is a strength of *Common Worship*, but it's also one of its greatest weaknesses: a Eucharistic Prayer for every day of the week, with three to spare, multiple confessions, affirmations of faith, congregational prayers after communion, and so on. The danger here is that by using too many texts and repeating fewer and fewer of them regularly, we are emptying our spiritual knap-sacks. This isn't good for us; and it's not good for those who are exploring the faith, for whom frequently used memorable texts with deep spiritual roots can provide a valuable resource for formation.

Related to this is the presentation of texts, which includes booklets, screens, one-off orders of service and whichever format worshippers might encounter them in. To take further the idea that worship is drama, those who go to the theatre or a concert are unlikely to take the script or the score with them. For to do so is to impoverish their participation in, and appreciation of, the performance. Their eyes are on the page rather than on the stage. And if that's true for drama that is entertainment, why should it not be even more true for worship that is the primary vocation of the Church?

Some may argue that by printing every word in a book or projecting it on a screen, participation is being enabled. But it's possible that the opposite is being achieved. The task of those who preside at worship is to get people's heads out of the booklets, or away from the screens, so that with open hearts and minds they can actively and expectantly participate in the drama of salvation, and so be drawn into the mystery of God.

The Liturgical Commission puts it like this in its commentary on the initiation services:

> Leading people in worship is leading people into the mystery, into the unknown and yet the familiar; this spiritual activity is much more than getting the words or the sections in the right order. The primary object in the careful planning and leading of the service is the spiritual direction which enables the whole congregation to come into the presence of God to give him glory, and then to go out energized for mission.[10]

This leads very naturally to the role of symbolism in recovering confidence in worship. Symbolism is part of the language of worship. Sandra Millar's research has revealed that it's the symbolic aspects of the infant baptism service that mean most to people, that they value and that stay with them after the event.[11]

A loss of confidence in the symbolic often expresses itself in not feeling able to let symbols speak for themselves, but rather to require explanation. 'And now we're going to make the sign of the cross on Charlie's forehead to show that . . .'; or 'And now we're going to give Molly a candle to symbolize that . . .' As soon as we explain the symbol, the symbolism is destroyed. It becomes mute. If we recall Cyril, Ambrose and Chrysostom, we see that the explanation came afterwards, in the mystagogy.

The suggestion here is not that, when preparing candidates for baptism, they shouldn't be told what's going to happen to them in the service. Far from it. Some of the most effective baptism preparation is based around the liturgy. Rather, during the celebration of the liturgy itself, at moments when explanation might be helpful, consideration should be given to doing it after rather than before the symbolic act; e.g. at the baptism of an infant, sign the candidate with the cross, and as parents and godparents are doing the same, talk about what is being done and why.

Conclusion

In recovering catechesis as an essential part of the life of the Church, it must not be forgotten that, as in the Church's earliest history, so too now, worship is an essential element of that catechesis.

It's essential for the candidates, in their being formed as disciples whose way of life authentically speaks of their faith, but it's also essential for the Christian community, providing them with an opportunity to express their support of those who wish to become partners with them within the household of faith, and reminding them of their own baptismal vocation and identity.

When it comes to the relationship between catechesis and worship, a silo mentality will never do. Looking for ways to recover a sense of confidence in worship will help the Church to integrate it with catechesis. A renewed confidence will allow catechesis and worship to transform each other, and to do so with the sole purpose of better enabling them to transform those who encounter them on their journey of faith.

For although the initial stage of catechesis may end with baptism and admission to communion, that part of catechesis that is mystagogy is a lifelong process in which, through worship, all Christians are continually being drawn deeper and deeper into the mystery of the God who, in Christ, unceasingly calls us to himself with the invitation to participate in the drama of salvation. There is no higher calling.

Notes

1 Tertullian, *On Baptism*, 20, E. C. Whitaker, *Documents of the Baptismal Liturgy*, revised and expanded edn, ed. Maxwell E. Johnson (London: SPCK, 2003), p. 11.

2 Alan Kreider, *The Change of Conversion and the Origin of Christendom* (Eugene, OR: Wipf & Stock, 1999) p. 41.

3 Cyril of Jerusalem, *Mystagogical Catechesis*, 2.5, Edward Yarnold, *The Awe-Inspiring Rites of Initiation* (Edinburgh: T&T Clark, 1994), p. 78.

4 Theodore of Mopsuestia, *Baptismal Homily*, 4.39, Yarnold, *The Awe-Inspiring Rites*.

5 Cyril of Jerusalem, *Mystagogical Catechesis*, 2.4, Yarnold, *The Awe-Inspiring Rites*.

6 Theodore of Mopsuestia, *Baptismal Homily*, 6.15, Yarnold, *The Awe-Inspiring Rites*, pp. 221–2.

7 Ambrose of Milan, *On the Sacraments*, 2.24, Yarnold, *The Awe-Inspiring Rites*, p. 119.

8 *Common Worship: Christian Initiation* (London: Church House Publishing, 2006), p. 10.

9 Sandra Millar, *Life Events* (London: Church House Publishing, 2018), p. 54.

10 *Common Worship: Christian Initiation*, p. 329.

11 Millar, *Life Events*, pp. 57–9.

4

Charismatic catechesis

CAROL HARRISON

The title of this chapter may sound a bit off-putting, so let me be clear what I mean by it. We tend to think of catechesis as the practice of giving instruction in the faith to those preparing for baptism or (now) confirmation. What I'd like to do in this chapter is to try to turn that traditional understanding on its head and to reflect on catechesis as first and foremost the practice, not of giving, but of *being given* the faith. In other words, I would like to think about catechesis, not as something that begins with us, but with God; not as something we somehow achieve through our own efforts, but something that we receive – or more precisely, which is inspired in us, by God. So, I would like to think about catechesis as, above all, a gift, a grace, a charism, given to both teacher and hearer – hence 'Charismatic Catechesis'.

Having turned it on its head, I'd then like to suggest that what we learn in catechesis is not so much a systematic understanding of 'what' God is, but rather we learn 'that' God is; that catechesis does not so much communicate *knowledge* of God as faith in and love of God; it is not so much a matter of the letter as of the spirit. The rules, creeds, conciliar definitions and doctrines that are usually associated with catechesis are therefore secondary, I suggest, to catechesis as an exercise in love; in participation and relation, with God, with Christ, with the Holy Spirit, the Church, and with one another. Whereas we normally think of catechesis as taking place through a clearly defined, formal process of teaching and hearing, I hope we will see that it can also take place through listening to scripture, through a common life and witness, through worship, praise and prayer, and through sacramental participation – in other words, through every aspect of Christian life.

What I would like to call 'charismatic catechesis' is summed up, I think, by one of Augustine of Hippo's (the fourth/fifth-century African bishop) favourite verses of scripture, Romans 5.5: 'The love of God is shed abroad in your hearts by the Holy Spirit which he has given to you.' Augustine cites this verse tirelessly and repeatedly, again and again, to make the point that God's gift of his Holy Spirit, which he sheds abroad in our hearts, is the only way in which we can come to know him, participate in him, and be united with him in faith, hope and love.

In this verse, the love of God, the Holy Spirit and God's gift or grace are effectively identified and made almost synonymous, in a way that is not only definitive of Augustine's thinking, but of the Western tradition that owes so much to him. In fact, this identification of love, Holy Spirit and grace is a rather revolutionary one, and a whole systematic theology follows from it: it first of all informs an understanding of God the Trinity, Father, Son and Holy Spirit, united in a threefold relation of begetting, being begotten and proceeding in love. It also informs a theological understanding of the whole of created reality and human existence, which comes into being through love, and is sustained, providentially ordered, reformed and saved through the loving operation and revelation of God the Trinity. We know this, Augustine insists, because we are part of this creation; created to be turned towards God in love; because we experience in our lives His providential loving action; and because, although sinful and fallen, his love is breathed into us, through the Holy Spirit, in order to inspire in us an answering love, by which we are turned once again to our Creator, to be formed and reformed in His image, revealed to us in his Son, and united in his body, the Church. Romans 5.5, and the way in which it was taken up into the Western tradition by a theologian such as Augustine, therefore presents us with a vision (I do not say understanding) of the faith that is inspired, informed and finds its means and end in the love that is God; a love that is from God, and returns us to God.

Unsurprisingly, another favourite quotation of Augustine's is
1 John 4.16: 'God is love, and he who dwells in love dwells in
God and God in Him.' Like Romans 5.5, this verse in a way
says everything that needs to be said. It expresses in a few words
what I have just tried to set out in terms of a systematic theology
based on love. In this context catechesis should be understood
as the practice of receiving, imparting, sharing and nurturing
this love; this gift and grace, which we can now appreciate is the
source, means and end of our faith, so that we are able to participate in it, and be united by it, with one another and with God.

Receiving God's grace: inspiration

In this chapter, I don't intend to elaborate on the various
aspects of what I have called a systematic theology of love. I
don't have space, but more importantly, as I suggested at the
beginning, I don't really need to, because, as we have seen,
what is important in catechesis is not an understanding of
what God is, as faith, hope and love, but *that* he is – and this is
not something we acquire, but rather something we are given.
What this means is that if catechesis is inspired and motivated
by love, then love – the lesson that it above all seeks to communicate – is already present and at work, informing and uniting
speaker and listener with each other and with God.

It is this process that I think the notion of inspiration
describes. Inspiration is not an easy idea to get to grips with
but in the early Church there was a firm and unwavering belief
in the inspiration of scripture by God, the Holy Spirit, so that
the whole of it, Old Testament and New Testament, was read
as the inerrant, infallible word of God. In one sense this sort of
approach to scripture is a bit of a stumbling block for modern
historical critical exegesis but I hope that what we have just
observed about the nature of love will go some way to making
it less alien and arbitrary than it might, at first, seem. The belief
that God, who *is* love, is the inspiration of the scriptures, is
really saying no more and no less than that the scriptures are

part of his redeeming grace, and that in every part they reveal him, by recounting his loving operation towards us. Augustine comments:

> Therefore the God-filled saints are inspired with the power of the Spirit, and the reason every scripture is said to be inspired by God, is that it is the teaching of the divine infusion of breath. If the bodily veil of the words is taken away, what remains is Sovereign and Life and Spirit, in accordance with great Paul and the Gospel saying. For Paul said that, for him who turns from the letter to the Spirit, what is apprehended is no longer the slavery that kills, but a Lord who is the lifegiving Spirit; and the sublime Gospel says, 'The words which I speak are Spirit and Life' (John 6.63), being stripped of their bodily veil.[1]

In a work on Christian teaching and learning entitled *On Christian Doctrine*, Augustine makes the radical claim that, in fact, we would not need scripture at all if we had already learned and taken to heart the one lesson that it teaches in every part: the lesson of faith, hope and – pre-eminently – love. He writes:

> Therefore a person strengthened by faith, hope and love, and who steadfastly holds on to them, has no need of the scriptures except to instruct others . . . When someone has learnt that the aim of the commandment is 'love from a pure heart, a good conscience and genuine faith' (1 Tim. 1.5), he will be ready to relate every interpretation of the holy scriptures to these three things and may approach the task of handling these books with confidence.[2]

Indeed, he suggests that the double commandment of love of God and love of neighbour is itself sufficient to interpret scripture and to establish the sense of a passage:

> So anyone who thinks that he has understood the divine scriptures or any part of them, but cannot by his understanding build up this double love of God and neighbour, has not

yet succeeded in understanding them. Anyone who derives from them an idea which is useful for supporting this love but fails to say what the writer demonstrably meant in the passage has not made a fatal error, and is certainly not a liar.[3]

So, when he turns to tackle the question of whether a particular text should be interpreted literally or spiritually – we might say according to the letter or the spirit – he asserts that if a text does not, in its literal sense – in other words in its obvious, plain sense – communicate the double commandment, then it should be interpreted spiritually, so that it does.

We must first explain the way to discover whether an expression is literal or figurative. Generally speaking, it is this: anything in the divine discourse that cannot be related either to good morals or to the true faith should be taken as figurative. Good morals have to do with our love of God and our neighbour, the true faith with our understanding of God and our neighbour.[4]

In other words, he appears to be suggesting that the literal sense of scripture must always be a lesson in love.

Is this sort of approach to scripture and its teaching simply to be dismissed as pre-critical, reductive and arbitrary, or can it still be appreciated for what I hope we have seen that, in essence, it is: a lesson in love – in other words, a lesson in the nature of God and an inspired communication of the message and meaning of the faith? This might prompt us to reflect once again on whether what matters in catechesis is primarily the letter or the spirit; statements, rules and formulae, or the communication of and participation in, the love of God?

Imparting God's grace: teaching and listening

Augustine answers this question directly in the preface of his *On Christian Doctrine*. He is responding to those who ask why we need scripture, or human teaching and preaching, at all, when God could have presumably simply inspired some-one directly, or at least, could have communicated with them through an angelic mediator, rather than a fallible human one. His answer to them is interesting and comes back to our point that what is important in catechesis is not so much *what* is taught as *that* it is taught. He observes: 'There would be no way for love, which ties people together in the bonds of unity, to make souls overflow and as it were intermingle with each other, if human beings learned nothing from other humans.'[5]

Likewise, he appeals to the common human experience of sharing something we know well with someone who is unfamiliar with it, so that we appreciate it through their eyes; we see it anew, and in the process are brought into a closer bond with them. This is how communicating the faith works: 'For so great is the power of sympathy,' he comments, 'that when people are affected by us as we speak and we by them as they learn, we dwell in one another and thus both they, as it were, speak in us what they hear, while we, after a fashion, learn in them what we teach.'[6]

That last quotation comes from a work in which Augustine reflects specifically on the practice of teaching and learning, his *De Catechizandis Rudibus*, which is usually translated as *On Teaching the Uninstructed*, or *Instructing Beginners in the Faith*. It is a work that puts what we have seen him observing in the Prologue of *On Christian Doctrine*, about the empathy that unites teacher and listener, into practice, and in the process gives us an extraordinary insight into Augustine's own practi-cal experience of teaching and his profound sensitivity to what is required in order to communicate and engage with a hearer effectively. Once again, he presents teaching and learning as an exercise and lesson in love, made possible by the love of God, which first inspires teacher and hearer, and which is also the means by which it is communicated, and the message itself. Augustine is clearly convinced that teaching and learning are only effective when inspired by love; when the motivation of the teacher is love; when the response of the hearer is love; and when what is communicated and received *is* love; so that speaker and listener are united in a participation in the love that is the source, the means, the message and the goal of their relationship.

This may all sound well and good, but just a bit vague. What it requires in practice is that the speaker or teacher or, in our case, the catechist, must, before they speak, first turn towards God in prayer in order to receive what they will say; in other words, as Augustine puts it, they must be an *orator*, one who prays, before they become a *dictor*, one who speaks.[7] The source of their words, like those of scripture, is therefore the inspiration of God. It also, in practice, requires a speaker who is not daunted by the challenge of having to put what they directly and readily grasp inwardly, within their heart and mind, into spoken or written words that inevitably and frustratingly, always fall short of expressing it – though this is hardly surprising given that their subject is the transcendent and ineffable God. Despite the difficulties the preacher or teacher faces – and despite their all too human tendency sometimes to feel unwilling and unworthy to speak; or simply too tired, depressed and demoralized, Augustine is clear that what primarily hinders their teaching is not so much their words as their motivation: if they do not teach in love, they will not be heard in love; if they do not delight in what they teach, they will not be heard with delight – and without love and delight nothing will be effectively communicated or understood. We have all had this experience, of course, both as speakers and listeners, and Augustine does not for a moment suggest that love and delight is something we can manufacture or acquire, rather it is given to us: first, by God's gracious inspiration, in response to our prayers; secondly by the message that we are given to communicate: the message of his creating, redeeming love, which cannot but occasion delight and love in those who hear and receive it.

Sharing God's grace: prayer and humility

What we now need to ask is: how do we receive this message and motivation of love, which is the source and substance of the faith, so that we can communicate it? We have just seen Augustine suggesting that the one who speaks must first be one who prays, acknowledging, in characteristic fashion, that all that we have we owe to the gracious gift of God's grace – and this includes not only our inward apprehension of the faith in our minds and hearts; our motivation to communicate it; our delight in it; but also the very words in which we express it. This leads us to another characteristic feature of Augustine's thinking that I think might also help us answer the question of just how it is we receive the message and motivation of love: this is his emphasis on humility: 'what do you have that you did not receive?' (1 Cor. 4.7)

I suspect I am not the only one who finds that, once I become self-conscious, once I start to feel uncertain about whether I am up to the task of teaching or preaching, or indeed, lecturing, once I try to be clever and impress, words dry up; they become stilted and incoherent – worse still, the person who has to listen to me looks bored, distracted or confused and certainly not fired by love and delight – precisely because I am no longer communicating my own love and delight in what I am saying. I think that we saw the opposite of this and witnessed what truly inspired teaching looks like when we all listened to the sermon preached at the wedding of Prince Harry and Megan Markle in 2018. A lot has subsequently been written about Bishop Michael Curry's sermon, and of course, it is not part of our culture to be so at ease and adept at delivering a sermon that feels extempore, open to improvisation, and that exploits rhetoric to stir and mould the souls of our listeners. This doesn't really matter. What really matters, I think, was Bishop Michael's humility: he was not imposing himself or his own ideas; he was not trying to be clever; rather, he had clearly thrown himself upon God; abandoned himself to his inspiration. The love of God was shed abroad in his heart by the Holy Spirit and that Spirit spoke loudly and clearly in his words. He preached on love, with a blazing love that caught his listeners up into the Spirit that blew through him (despite a few raised eyebrows and incredulous smiles), and all were united in love of God. That, for me, is precisely what Augustine had in mind in *On Christian Doctrine* and *On Teaching Beginners in the Faith*.

But I must not get carried away. Despite first impressions, this type of teaching and preaching – or catechizing and being catechized – is far from being a wild, charismatic moment of throwing ourselves upon God. It may be inspired by love, guided by the Spirit, open to extemporizing, but it is also, importantly, a matter of spiritual discipline. As we have seen, it depends on, and is the fruit of, meditation upon scripture and of prayer. It depends on practice – not just the practice of speaking extempore (that can be learned) – but the practice of prayer and meditation.

One way of illustrating this is to think of a moment when you have been so caught in up in what you are reading, thinking, or doing that you have lost any sense of time, or place, or self: time stands still; place is of no account; we forget ourselves. These are liberating moments, when exciting things happen: our attention doesn't wander; we are completely wrapped up in what we are doing; we think and speak and act in a way that has nothing to do with us and everything to do with what we are attending to and which consumes us. They are undistracted, single-minded moments; moments when we become what we attend to.

It was from such a moment, I think, that Bishop Michael's sermon arose, but we can all have them. They are the moments that he was, in fact, describing: moments of love, when we forget ourselves, abandon ourselves, act freely, unselfconsciously, spontaneously; when we are inspired, consumed, drawn by the object of our love. They are moments that we don't control, or deliberate over, or rationalize; rather they are the moments when we pray or read or meditate. They are also, of course, the moments when we write poetry or compose music; the moments when we knit, or watch children playing; the moments when we dance or fall in love, and ideally, they are the moments in which we teach and preach – catechize and are catechized – effectively.

This single-minded, single-hearted focus on God was what early Christians described as the discipline of asceticism – of self-denial, of prayer, and of turning away from attachment to the world or to sinful habits, in order to be turned wholly towards God.

Augustine described this all-consuming movement of love, which is the movement of grace within us, with the memorable image of love as a weight – or what we would now call a gravitational force: 'My weight is my love,' he says, 'wherever I go my love is what brings me there . . . As the mind is carried by its love, so is the body by its weight; each to its own place . . . fire goes up, a stone comes down . . . oil floats on water . . . My weight is my love; by it I move wherever I move.'[8]

Love is not something we direct but which directs us; it is something we receive, which works within us, and draws us inexorably towards God, who is its source. If, in single-mindedly directing our lives towards him through such things as the practice of reading and prayer, worship and meditation, we allow ourselves to be caught up in and inspired by that love, then our teaching and preaching, our catechizing and being catechized, cannot but be effective.

Nurturing God's grace: confession of faith, worship and sacramental participation

It might well be asked if this leaves any space for what we traditionally understand as catechesis: the exercise of teaching the faith to candidates for baptism, in certain set forms and practices, in preparation for their sacramental initiation. In the early Church the Lord's Prayer, the creed or some other summary statement of the faith would be delivered to those who were preparing for Christian initiation in baptism through catechetical lectures or sermons, delivered over a period of time – sometimes a number of years, but at least during the course of Lent – culminating in the moment when the candidates were ready publicly to profess their faith by handing back, or reciting, the creed that had been handed over to them. Until they were baptized, the mysteries of the Eucharist were kept from them, and only after baptism and their first communion were these described and explained. This is what formal catechesis looks like.

But in practice, catechesis has always involved far more than simply teaching and being taught. The period of preparation, while candidates for baptism were still officially called catechumens, was one in which they learned and practiced the spiritual disciplines we have just described: prayer, meditation on scripture, and in the early Church, confession of sins, spiritual guidance, exorcisms, fasting, celibacy. So catechetical instruction was a matter for the body as well as the mind; for the heart as well as the intellect, designed to prepare the candidates to receive the sanctifying, saving grace of the Holy Spirit in baptism. The actual ceremony of baptism was also as much a matter of bodily actions and practice as of teaching. Perhaps more than ever, what was done mattered far more than what was said. It was a drama that not only enacted salvation but caught the participants up into it. Salvation history, turning from evil to good, sin to righteousness, the old man to the new man, was played out in an elaborate choreography of physical actions and material symbols: processions, anointings, candles, nakedness and white garments, turning west and east, threefold immersion in water . . . were all a means, not only of enacting but of effecting, salvation.

I say this to stress what I suggested earlier: that what matters in catechesis is not so much *what* is said as *that* it is said. The practices of the catechumenate, the dramatic actions and rituals of baptism, are all examples of those aspects of catechesis that initiated catechumens not only into *what* the faith is, but *that* it is; they enabled them not only to cognize it but to participate in it and be transformed by it.

This is something that we see at the forefront of the arguments that Gregory of Nyssa, one of Augustine's Eastern contemporaries, rehearses against those who thought that they could actually capture and define God's very being in words – in this case, they thought they could define God's substance as 'unbegotten' or 'uncaused'. In response, Gregory and his fellow bishops in Cappadocia, Basil of Caesarea and Gregory Nazianzen (the Cappadocians), argued that God's transcendent, infinite, limitless nature was both unknowable and ineffable to human beings. They stressed that whatever we can affirm about God relates not to his divine nature but to his revelation and activities towards us – in prophecy, salvation history, the incarnation, the operation of the Holy Spirit, the Church and sacraments.

The titles or names we give God, therefore, come from his actions towards us, rather than his nature:

> For my part, taught by divinely inspired scripture, this is what I boldly declare: He who is above every name becomes many-named for us, with titles according to his various acts of kind-ness, Light when he abolishes the darkness of ignorance, Life when he bestows immortality, Way when he guides us from error to truth; so too Strong Tower, Fenced City, Fountain, Rock, Vine, Physician, Resurrection, and all such names are given to him in relation to us, distributing himself variously between his benefits to us.[9]

In other words, the Cappadocians firmly believed that we cannot state *what* God is, only *that* he is, on the basis of his actions towards us (Gregory comments that trying to grasp the divine nature in words is like trying to hold the sea in the palm of one's hand).[10]

They equally affirmed – against those who were teaching that all that was necessary for a Christian was correct doctrine, rather than sacraments and worship – that the only adequate human response to God's unknowable, ineffable divine nature, was indeed worship, what Gregory calls the 'sacramental symbols' and 'ceremonies of the Church'.[11] They insisted that what was required was not only correct dogma, but prayer, praise, confession of faith, and sacramental participation in the mysteries of baptism and Eucharist. Here, they asserted, we can encounter, participate in, and be formed and reformed by the transcendent God, without the need for doctrinal definitions. As Gregory comments, 'Those therefore who in practice deny the faith, despise the ceremonies, disregard the confession of the names, and judge the sanctification coming from the sacramental signs as worth nothing, but are persuaded to look to cunningly devised words, and think that salvation lies in the verbal logic of "begotten" and "unbegotten", what else are they but transgressors against the doctrines of salvation?'[12]

But we should not misunderstand them: the Cappadocians were agreed that creeds, summaries, doctrinal statements and definitions are indeed helpful and instructive in catechesis, but only if we remember that they are very much beginnings, not ends; that they are statements of faith in what cannot be fully known by human reason; expressions of the limitations of human knowing in relation to the unknowable, ineffable God; the best that fallen and fallible human beings, assisted by divine inspiration and grace, can do in gesturing towards the transcendent God. They are not definitive statements that pin him down for rational analysis.

One important result of this realization is that the divide between teacher and pupil, catechist and catechized, is to a large extent elided, for both are human beings before God; both are entirely dependent on God's gracious inspiration and revelation for whatever they are able to learn of him; and the lesson that both learn is not what God is, but that God is: pre-eminently, they learn that God is love, and insofar as we love, we know and are united with God and one another. Catechesis, or initiation into the faith, is therefore not a higher knowledge or insight to be taught by an educated or spiritual elite, but something that all, educated and uneducated, literate and illiterate, receive in devout humility, prayer, praise, confession of faith and sacramental participation.

If we tried to capture what such a confession of faith might look like, it would not be a set of definitions or categorical statements, but more like Julian of Norwich's description of the Revelation of Divine Love:

Do you wish to know your Lord's meaning in this thing? Know it well, love was his meaning. Who reveals it to you? Love. What did he reveal to you? Love. Why does he reveal it to you? For love. Remain in this and you will know more of the same. But you will never know different, without end. So I was taught that love is our Lord's meaning. And I saw very certainly in this and in everything that before God made us he loved us, which love has never abated and never will be. And in this love he has done all his works, and in this love he has made all things profitable to us, and in this love our life is everlasting.[13]

So I would like us to recognize that all that we do as Christians – our teaching, preaching, reading and listening to scripture, our common worship, our private and communal prayer, our sacraments – are all means of catechesis; of incorporating people into the body of Christ, through the Spirit, to worship God the Trinity. This is also what it is to practice catechesis: it is not something separate from other forms of Christian devotion, but rather sums them up by informing them: it is the grace of God shed abroad in our hearts by the Holy Spirit. We must become sounding chambers for this love, resonating, echoing, repeating, responding through our preaching, teaching, prayer, confession of faith, praise and worship, so that all can be caught up with us in the love of God that is God, and become of one heart and one mind in God.

Notes

1 Gregory of Nyssa, *Against Eunomius*, 3.5.15–16 in Johan Leemans and Matthieu Cassin, eds, Stuart G. Hall, trans., Gregory of Nyssa: *Contra Eunomium* III An English Translation with Commentary and Supporting Studies. Proceedings of the 12th International Colloquium on Gregory of Nyssa. Supplements of *Vigiliae Christianae* 124 (Leiden, Boston: Brill, 2010).

2 Augustine, *On Christian Doctrine*, 1.39.43–40.44, D. W. Robertson, trans., Library of Liberal Arts 80 (Indianapolis: Bobbs-Merrill, 1958).

3 *On Christian Doctrine*, 1.36.40.

4 *On Christian Doctrine*, 3.10.14.

5 *On Christian Doctrine*, Prologue 6, 8.

6 Augustine, *On Teaching Beginners in the Faith*, 12, in Raymond Canning, trans., *Works of Saint Augustine* 1.10 (Hyde Park, NY: New City Press, 2006).

7 *On Christian Doctrine*, 4.15.32; 4.30.63.

8 Augustine, *Confessions*, 13.9.10, in Maria Boulding, trans., *Works of Saint Augustine* 1.1 (Hyde Park, NY: New City Press, 1997).

9 Gregory of Nyssa, *Against Eunomius*, 3.8.10.

10 *Against Eunomius*, 3.5.53–55.

11 *Against Eunomius*, 3.10.54–60.

12 *Against Eunomius*, 3.10.60.

13 Julian of Norwich, *Showings*, Edmund Colledge and James Walsh, trans., *The Classics of Western Spirituality* (London: SPCK, 1978), p. 86.

5

Making Christians and lifelong catechesis

JENNIFER STRAWBRIDGE

Introduction

Writing in the second century, a Christian convert named Tertullian proclaimed that 'Christians are made, not born.'[1] As Simon Jones and Carol Harrison have argued, Christianity is not simply a body of knowledge that one needs to acquire in order to have faith; Christianity is a way of life that one embodies. Thus, catechesis or Christian formation encompasses both knowledge and ethics; catechesis embraces both teaching and action, both belief and behaviour. Catechesis is the process of making Christians.

Catechesis literally means 'to echo' or 'to resound'. And what is echoed or sounded forth is none other than the teaching and life of Jesus. The goal of catechesis thus includes both knowledge of the good news, the gospel, of Jesus Christ and the echoing of Jesus in this world and following his command to 'go therefore and make disciples of all nations' which includes 'teaching them to obey everything that I have commanded you' (Matt. 28.19–20). In other words, Jesus calls his followers to action, action that includes teaching.

Numerous early Christian writers confirm this understanding of catechesis as active instruction. The great third-century bishop and martyr Cyprian proclaims: 'We do not preach great things, we live them.'[2] Early Christians from Tertullian to

Augustine are clear that they can identify Christians when they 'see how they love one another'. Even the concrete teaching in one of the earliest catechetical documents we have, called the *Didache*, is focused not only on scripture and theology, but also on instruction in humility, charity, gentleness, and other moral elements that ought to accompany the Christian life.

But as good as this kind of formation sounds, what we now want to know is what was the content that makes up this early Christian preaching and teaching? What was the instruction that transformed both belief and behaviour? What can we learn from the earliest Christians and then apply to how we instruct others in the faith today?

Unfortunately, early Christian writers did not leave us an outline of their teaching in a neat six-week programme ready for us to use in our parishes. In fact, very few wrote down any semblance of a clear programme for catechumens, for those who were being instructed in the Christian faith. And my hunch is that this isn't because a programme didn't exist, but rather because catechesis was not something that ever ended. For early Christians, formation was a lifelong process and thus catechesis didn't stop at baptism and couldn't be shoehorned into a few meetings. And while debates rage over whether we can know anything about the specific content of early Christian catechesis, early Christians didn't leave us without any guidance for formation. We just have to know where to look.

Catechesis and scripture

Our starting point for Christian formation is scripture. The study of scripture was an essential element of early Christian instruction. This link is confirmed by some of the earliest references to catechumens, which are found in early Christian letters. These letters, preserved by the dry climate of the Egyptian desert and found on what is thought to be an ancient rubbish heap, introduce us to a figure called Papa Sotas. We know from numerous other writings in this period that one title of address for teachers was 'Papa' and thus he is most likely an early Christian teacher. Within the letters to this ancient teacher, we encounter a man named Anos who was 'a catechumen in Genesis',[3] and another 'catechumen in the beginning of the gospel'.[4] In other words, some of the earliest descriptions of people being taught in the Christian faith emphasize the centrality of scripture – from Genesis to the Gospels – in this endeavour.

Something else that we glean from these letters, which we will return to later in this chapter, is the personal connection that these catechumens had with their teachers, both those who send them to Papa Sotas and the welcome the letter writer hopes they will receive. The instruction offered by these teachers doesn't appear to be in a large classroom with a lecturer at the front, as we so often think of teaching and learning today, but is on an individual basis and appears to be tailored to the needs of those being formed.

Returning to the theme of scripture, the centrality of the biblical texts in Christian formation may seem like an obvious point. Scripture narrates the fundamental story of salvation and the relationship between God and God's creation which sets the standard that Christians seek to embody and enact. But the Bible is not a small text as it consists of dozens of books, hundreds of chapters, and thousands of stories. So where are we to focus our instruction in scripture? How can scripture with all of its breadth help us to encourage others in their belief and their behaviour? To start to address these questions, we begin with the earliest Christian writings that we have: the letters of the Apostle Paul.

The letters of the Apostle Paul

The 13 letters that are attributed to Paul make up almost half of the books in the New Testament. Written only 20 to 30 years after the death of Jesus, Paul is addressing a number of specific situations and questions raised by some of the earliest followers of Christ. These issues range from life after death to lawsuits, from marriage to idolatry. Paul's writings are significant not only for their early date and the particular issues they engage, but these letters also have a tremendous influence on Christian writers in the early centuries of the Church. Within the Bible itself, we find Paul's letters counted among 'the scriptures' even if in the same breath they are also declared as 'hard to understand' (2 Pet. 3.16).

Paul's own identity and mission serves as an example for early Christian writers. Paul has only one source and focus: the proclamation of the gospel and its power to transform lives. Paul sees himself as an apostle 'set free for the gospel of God' (Rom. 1.1) and this gospel is the 'power of God for salvation' (Rom. 1.16). Teaching and proclaiming the gospel of God is Paul's primary concern (1 Cor. 9.23; Gal. 2.5) and yet the gospel is not simply the content of his instruction, it is also what leads to the transformation of lives.

Of course, Paul's primary example of this transformation is his own life. As he briefly recounts his transformation by Christ and his becoming an apostle, Paul prays that others will be able to imitate him and experience the saving power of the gospel. Paul does not need to write another gospel or even recount most of the gospel story, instead he lives the gospel, the good news of Christ's life, death, and resurrection. Once again, as in the letters to Papa Sotas, we see the personal connection between the teacher and his or her life and those who are being transformed by the good news of God.

It is no wonder then that the writings and the person of Paul are substantial influences on early Christians. Paul's words undergird early Christian homilies, defences of the faith (called 'apologies'), treatises, and commentaries. How early Christians use Paul's writings helps us to paint a picture of the content of early Christian instruction and the ethics such teaching demanded. While the specific details concerning the content of teaching and catechesis in the first few centuries of Christianity are almost impossible to determine, scripture and its use in early Christian writings gives us a sense of what early Christians taught. And more than this, through their use of scripture such as the writings of Paul, we can begin to understand how the use of a particular passage contributed to Christian formation and identity. One way that we can thus draw out some of the specifics of early Christian formation is to look at some of the most frequently used passages of scripture across early Christian writings. And the texts from Paul's letters that come up time and again, across regions and centuries of Christian teaching, point us to the parts of scripture that were important for this teaching.

Early Christian catechesis and Paul's letters

1 Corinthians 2

The most popular Pauline text among early Christians is a section from chapter two of Paul's first letter to the Corinthians. Throughout this letter, Paul is addressing the specific concerns of a community who seem to be in an adolescent-like phase of their Christian formation. Among other things, they are worried about food, self-image, sex, relationships, and death. But from the start, they are also worried about wisdom and knowledge, to the point that claiming a lot of both of these things is something they lord over and use against each other. Paul is concerned that the Corinthian Christians continue to grow in wisdom. He certainly isn't advocating ignorance. But the wisdom he proclaims is not the wisdom of this world, which they seem to be most concerned about, but the wisdom of God. Within 1 Corinthians 2, therefore, we find Paul encouraging his community to differentiate between worldly wisdom and the wisdom of God. He wants them to be more concerned with 'God's wisdom, secret and hidden' that he teaches them, rather than 'a wisdom that is of this age or of the rulers of this age' (1 Cor. 2.6–7). But what precisely does this mean for catechesis?

Early Christian writers, eager to harness the wisdom of Paul and use it against their opponents, latch onto Paul's statement about the 'secret and hidden' wisdom that is God's. And this leads to one of the earliest understandings of the purpose of Christian formation. According to early Christians, teachers should help followers of Christ – new and old – to grow in wisdom. Practically this means that some who are exploring the Christian faith come to it with no knowledge of the wisdom of God but lots of worldly wisdom. Others might be in the process of formation with a completely different level of wisdom – that of this world and that of God. Thus, early Christians, like a prolific second-century teacher named Origen, concluded that people with different kinds of wisdom needed different kinds of formation.

Such a conclusion sounds like a good reminder for the Church today: that different kinds of Christian formation are needed and there isn't one simple approach that will speak to everyone who is seeking to grow in wisdom. Such a conclusion also gives us a clear understanding of Christian formation and its purpose: it is the movement from one level of wisdom to another. Formation is growing in wisdom. The only problem is that such language leads us to believe that we need advanced degrees in theology or that we need to speak in high and lofty words in order to communicate this wisdom.

Certainly, preparation for teaching and formation by all of those involved in the process is essential. Certainly, we will have to engage theology – which is simply the study of God. But Paul himself helps us to see that our assumptions about this wisdom are misplaced. For he is clear that he did not approach the Corinthians 'proclaiming the mystery of God to you in lofty words', but rather, Paul 'decided to know nothing among you except Jesus Christ and him crucified' (1 Cor. 2.1–2).

For a number of early Christian writers, this statement by Paul encompasses the most essential element of catechesis: to teach and to know Jesus Christ and him crucified. This is the beginning of wisdom and the basic level of Christian teaching, preaching, and formation. This is the starting point of Christian formation. And the very existence of a starting point means that catechesis is not stagnant. Formation is a movement into deeper levels of wisdom, taking us on a journey of knowledge and growth that doesn't have an obvious end. The wisdom of God, which is the wisdom to which Paul and all early Christians aspire, is acquired through the Holy Spirit, through knowledge of the scriptures, and with the help of a preacher and teacher who can preach and teach the essential message of Christ crucified and guide Christians into deeper wisdom. Thus, the fundamental understanding of Christian teaching and catechesis which we can continue to embody today is this movement from one level of wisdom to another. And yet, Christian formation is not only about knowledge and wisdom but is also a transformation of all of life shaped by Jesus Christ and him crucified.

Ephesians 6

Thus, we turn to the second popular Pauline text among early Christians, a graphic section of the letter to the Ephesians. Here we find descriptions of wrestling, battle, and the armour of God. And here we bump up against the reality that growing in wisdom centred on Christ is a very good thing, but that this very good thing does not mean the Christian life is without struggle or ethical demands. Such struggle, according to Ephesians, concerns all kinds of forces including 'rulers', 'authorities', 'cosmic powers of this present darkness', and 'spiritual forces of wickedness in the heavenly places' (Eph. 6.12). Against all of this evil and the things that can cause us harm in this life, Ephesians 6 offers the concrete command that Christians are to 'take up the whole armour of God' (6.13).

Now before we get nervous about this language of armour and battle, we need to learn more about what this gear actually is. For the armour of God includes all the bits one might expect: shield, breastplate, sword, helmet. Except these are now equated to the attributes of truth, righteousness, peace, faith, salvation, the Spirit, and the word of God (6.14–17) and in a context in which the Ephesians are exhorted to pray 'at

all times in every prayer and supplication' (6.18). Alongside
the language of battle, we find front and centre the importance
of prayer, faith, and standing firm in the midst of temptation
and attack by forces of wickedness. Catechesis in this sense is
not simply an exercise in knowledge of Christ, but is the very
embodiment of him. It is a lived reality.

Within this context, the familiar language of physical war-
fare is used to describe not a physical battle, but a spiritual
one, especially at moments of vulnerability. And for many of
the early Christians who used this passage in their sermons and
other writings, the most vulnerable moment for a Christian
was the moment of baptism. Baptism is the moment when one
makes a life-changing and life-transforming decision to stand
firmly with Christ. Baptism is the moment when one decides to
'know nothing except Jesus Christ and him crucified'. And baptism is the moment when temptation is greatest to turn back to
one's former life and to not embrace the change that the identity as 'Christian' brings. Certainly formation is about growing
in wisdom and knowledge of Jesus Christ and of scripture. But
the ethical injunctions to prayer and faith are concrete ways
that Christians can maintain faith in a world that questions it
and stand fast in God's wisdom in a world that values other
kinds of wisdom and knowledge.

Catechesis is thus a process of formation in which we are
to grow in the wisdom of God, based on Jesus Christ and
grounded in the scriptures, but alongside such growth comes
the mandate to baptism and to prayer. But for many of us at
this point, the content of this wisdom and who Jesus Christ
is remains unclear. And so we must turn to another highly
used passage in early Christian writings, a passage about Jesus
Christ himself, found in the letter to the Colossians.

Colossians 1

Within the Pauline letter to the people of Colossae, we encounter claims about Christ that influenced the writing of the Nicene

Creed that we still say today as our profession of faith. Within Colossians 1, a number of titles are attributed to Jesus who is the 'image of the invisible God, the firstborn of all creation; for in him all things in heaven and on earth were created' (Col. 1.15–16).

Such claims about Jesus sound familiar and uncontroversial to us today, but these words are some of the most radical statements within scripture, closely connected to the words at the beginning of John's Gospel proclaiming that the Word who 'was God' is also the Word who 'became flesh' (John 1.3, 14). When we look at the claims in Colossians, we think back to the experience of Moses in the Old Testament and the statement in John's Gospel that 'no one has ever seen God' (John 1.18). And yet Colossians makes clear that all of this changes with the incarnation, when God becomes human. We are thus told that while God the Father remains invisible, while we cannot see the Father, Jesus is the image of this invisible God and thus reveals God to us in a whole new way. Jesus as the image of God means that we can know something of the unknowable, infinite, invisible God because this God has been made visible with us. Jesus Christ, who is the content of all wisdom and knowledge in our teaching, is the one who embodies God. Jesus, as God's image, means that to see and hear and receive Jesus is to see and hear and receive God.

In this way, while the content of our catechesis is Jesus Christ and him crucified, and the demands that such wisdom places upon us are ethical, changing us through our baptism, prayer, faith, and reading of scripture, Colossians gives us another dimension of formation. For we are not only called to see and receive the person of Christ in our lives, but we are called to imitate Christ. And this imitation means that we are called to make God and God's love visible and tangible in our broken and divided world. Just as Christ made God and God's love visible to us in the incarnation, so we, too, are called to make God present. And my sense is that we all have stories of sacred moments where this has happened in or through us, most prominently in the sacrament of the Eucharist, and in other ways as well.

Serving as a chaplain in a large Roman Catholic hospital and trauma unit outside New York City, one morning I encountered three children who had been in a horrendous car accident on their way to school. One child was blinded by glass, one was in critical condition, and the other died at the hospital. In such a situation, there are no words that can be spoken. And yet days after sitting with the family in the moment when the doctor told them their child had died, offering water, a phone, and a prayer of commendation for the young child, a note arrived to give thanks for the many words of wisdom and prayer offered in that time – words I know I did not speak. Such experience speaks to the power of presence and the power of making visible that which is not.

Jesus as the image of God shows us that sharing God's Word and moving from one level of wisdom to another in formation is not only about words, it is also about Jesus made present to us in one another and especially in the sacrament. We are such a verbal culture that we can understand Jesus Christ as God made visible, as God's Word made flesh in the world, and we like to proclaim Jesus as Word. But there is also the element of Jesus as God's image which means we don't have to have words for every situation. We don't have to explain all of God's mystery. Rather God's presence, God's visibility can speak louder than words, if we will let it.

And this leads us into one of the great mysteries of Christian faith, which we find in Colossians and throughout the New Testament: Christ crucified, who shares the authority and nature of God, is also 'the head of the body, the Church' and 'the firstborn from the dead' (Col. 1.18). In other words, the Christ we proclaim, the Christ who is the basic foundation of our teaching, is Christ crucified *and* risen.

1 Corinthians 15

That we are called to proclaim Christ crucified and risen leads us to one final favourite passage of scripture used in early

Christian writings: a portion of 1 Corinthians 15 on resurrection. For resurrection is an essential element of Christian teaching as well. Christ as 'firstborn from the dead' as we find in Colossians is significant because it highlights the uniqueness of Christ's resurrection as a singular event in the past. But such language is also the guarantee of resurrection for those who follow Christ, growing in wisdom and faith. For Jesus as 'firstborn' suggests that more will follow. What 1 Corinthians 15 adds to the understanding of resurrection is that this resurrection, as defended by early Christians using this Pauline letter, is not simply of the soul or the spirit, but is a resurrection of the whole body. While early Christians are concerned about the content of wisdom, the person of Christ, and the manifestations of faith in baptism and in prayer, they are also concerned to affirm the value of the body as the medium of salvation. Thus, the ethical demand placed on Christians also involves the body because it is the locus of the incarnation and of salvation; it is the place wherein the Word became flesh. With this understanding then, catechesis included both formation in Christ and the scriptures, but also, necessarily, included moral education.

Catechesis and formation

Catechesis includes knowledge and ethics; it is about belief and behaviour. Christian formation involves knowledge of and immersion in the words of scripture alongside knowledge and immersion in the Word of God, Jesus. Christian formation is growing in the wisdom of God and of Christ and him crucified. Christian formation is knowing the significance of the body as the locus of incarnation, resurrection, and salvation and embodying Christ in our very being. Christian formation is being grounded in faith and knowing that this faith is a gift from God; it is immersion in prayer and offering intercession for ourselves and our world. Christian formation is baptism into the death and resurrection of Christ, a moment that marks not the end, but the beginning of a new catechesis, the beginning of a life that echoes Christ.

All of these dimensions – Christ, wisdom, prayer, faith, baptism, presence, resurrection – make up the focus of early Christian writings on formation. Based on the letters of St Paul, we can begin to create a picture of the Christian identity that catechesis sought to create. For the identity of the Christian that emerges from these texts is one who is imbued with wisdom, embattled, raised with Christ at the end of time, and with faith in the one who is fully human, fully divine, the image of God who is crucified, risen, and co-creator with God the Father.

This identity, this setting apart that begins with the differentiation between levels of wisdom, suggests that early Christians were aware that they were different, special, and could sit at odds with the wisdom of this world and the conventions of wider society. This movement towards God and God's wisdom suggests that formation implicitly demands progress and a journey of knowledge and transformation that has no obvious terminus. The reality that we cannot achieve full wisdom, absolute perfection, protection from all struggle and evil, and ultimately the Kingdom of God in this world, suggests that Christian identity is that of a lifelong catechumen, informed by a sense of journey.

Even in the New Testament examples of those who are baptized at the moment of conversion (see Acts 8 and 10) do not suggest that catechesis, the teaching of the faith, stops at the moment of baptism. Rather at that moment, the one baptized becomes a disciple, a student of the gospel and a part of the community of faith. Those who are baptized at the moment of conversion do not have a fully mature and perfect faith. Rather they join a community comprised of people at all different levels of wisdom, but all seeking to grow deeper in their knowledge of Jesus Christ and him crucified and raised. One becomes a Christian at baptism, but the rest of our lives we are disciples of Christ, involved in the process of growing in wisdom and embodying Christ. And this process is called catechesis.

Except that catechesis as a lifelong process and teaching that continues even after baptism sounds like a lot of work.

How are we to maintain a curriculum that continues year upon year? How are we to adapt our teaching to people with all different levels of wisdom (not to mention expectations)? The good news is that catechesis is about more than a teacher and is not about endless classes and extra offerings.

Catechesis and community

Of course, at times we like to think that catechesis and formation revolves around us and that we can take the credit when someone grows in wisdom and in faith. Or we like to point to a moment when someone can say that 'I decided to become a Christian' or 'I accepted Jesus Christ', except that this isn't how catechesis, or faith for that matter, works. Faith isn't something that we decide to acquire or accept. For before we could get to a point of decision or acceptance, someone had to teach us the story of Jesus Christ and him crucified. Someone had to not only proclaim, but also to live out their faith before we could. Someone had to be there for us to imitate. For Paul, this person was Jesus. For many early Christians, this person was Paul, who embodied Jesus and the gospel.

What we have to remember is that a teacher is not simply someone who stands in front of a class and imparts knowledge and wisdom, but a teacher is also one who serves as an example for others to imitate. For early Christians, the content for their teaching and formation was found in Paul's gospel, but these words were exemplified in Paul's very person. Thus Paul does not just preach and teach Jesus Christ and him crucified and risen, but he carries 'the marks of Jesus branded' on his body (Gal. 6.17) and urges his communities to be 'imitators of me, as I am of Christ' (1 Cor. 11.1).

We find similar words throughout early Christian writings where one of the earliest bishops and martyrs, named Ignatius, exhorts Christians 'to imitate Jesus Christ as he imitated the Father'. And we are told that Origen taught not only knowledge of God but 'by his own moral behaviour' was 'an example of one who is wise'.[5] In other words, teaching the knowledge of Christ is essential, but living examples of what this means are especially effective. The highest praise that early Christians give to their teachers is that they were not simply taught about Christianity by lectures and words, but were shown how to live the Christian life by their teachers. It is perhaps no wonder that from about the third century, one popular tool for teaching the Christian life was through the stories of the lives of holy men and women.

The reality of Christian formation, therefore, is that even those who take on the role of teacher and preacher are being formed as they too grow in wisdom and seek to follow Christ. Moreover, teaching isn't confined to courses and programmes and classrooms but must be embodied in the life of the community to which all are invited. Catechesis is about individual Christians and their growth, but it is also about the Christian community as a whole. The Christian teacher, preacher, and priest offer leadership and scriptural explication and strive to follow the example of Christ. But such roles are only possible if others are present in the community to support this endeavour of growth.

One of the ways that the communal aspect of catechesis is made most tangible is through the language of armour from Ephesians 6, discussed earlier in this section. One key element of this armour is the 'shield of faith' which doesn't sound like much. Except when we realize that the particular kind of shield named in this letter is a very large shield that only covers half of a soldier's body. The other part of the shield covers the soldier's neighbour. In other words, one is extremely vulnerable if standing alone with this shield as half of their body is exposed. But in literal formation, in community with other soldiers standing side by side, all are protected. The demand on the Christian community therefore is to uphold one another in faith and to grow in wisdom both as individuals but also as part of a community. For through engaging a community, through moving from baptism deeper into the life of faith as a member of Christ's body, the Church, we each take on the role of helping others to grown in wisdom, making Christ present among us, sharing in Christ's body and blood, and helping to shield those who are most vulnerable since we never know what kind of battle those around us are fighting.

What such support might look like in practice we encounter in the story of the conversion of that great third-century bishop, Cyprian. Cyprian, we are told, had what he called a 'soul friend' named Caecilianus who accompanied him not only through his formation and baptism, but who continued to walk alongside him as a 'parent' of his life of faith. The relationship was so powerful for Cyprian that he commended his family's care to his soul friend when he was martyred. What this relationship between Cyprian and Caecilianus gives us is not only another example of how catechesis happens, but also makes the point that the Christian community is the locus of catechesis. Proclamation of the gospel and transformation begins in community. The same community welcomes those who wish to grow in wisdom. And this community is the focus of support when the struggles of life are too much to bear, including threat of martyrdom for many Christians still in our world today.

Conclusion

Early Christians offer us a number of models for our catechesis even today, commending to us the importance of teachers, but also making clear the importance of the whole community in formation. Catechesis draws together the formal instruction offered by the Church – instruction that includes preaching, young church, sacramental preparation, biblical study, and leadership training – with the informal sharing of wisdom and faith found within the context of a community.

The Apostle Paul as one of the first teachers of the faithfulness of and faith in Jesus Christ, influenced the foundation of Christian doctrine and many of the proclamations of faith that we still pray in the church today. But Paul, in his imitation of Christ and his focus on community, also set for us an example of Christian formation where belief and behaviour are closely connected and where catechesis and growth in the wisdom of God in Christ is a lifelong journey.

Returning to those words preached by Tertullian over 1800 years ago, 'Christians are made, not born', helps us to grasp that formation is not about helping others to dig deep, close their eyes, and believe. Formation is embodying Christ in our lives as an example to others, and giving them the tools and the story of faith, which were given to us, so they and we may continue to grow in wisdom.

And as early Christians who used Paul in their own teachings assert, growing in wisdom is not just about the delivering of facts about Jesus. As Paul makes clear, growing in wisdom is about the transformation of one's life to embody Jesus and his life. As such, we never come to the end of our need to grow in the wisdom that accompanies our ability to forgive, to be generous, to welcome the stranger, to do justice, to love mercy, and to walk with God. For formation must lead to transformation, enacted first in baptism and effected in community, in word and sacrament. Those who follow Jesus are lifelong disciples. Catechesis is not something that stops at baptism, but rather this is just the beginning.

Understanding catechesis as a lifelong journey where all are called to move to deeper levels of wisdom and knowledge of Jesus Christ means that the Church cannot be stagnant. Catechesis as progress and growth means the Church continually moves and thus can never be an organization of which one is a 'member'. Rather, the Church becomes an invitation, a movement, that is growing and changing in an unending process of proclaiming the gospel of Jesus Christ for none other than the transformation and redemption of our broken world.

Notes

1 Tertullian, *Apology*, 18.4.
2 Cyprian, *On Patience*, 3.

3 P. Oxy. 36.2785. For references to these letters and other early correspondence with Papa Sotas, see AnneMarie Luijendijk, *Greetings in the Lord: Early Christians and the Oxyrhynchus Papyri* (Cambridge: Harvard University Press, 2008).

4 PSI 9.1041, Luijendijk, *Greetings in the Lord.*

5 Gregory of Nyssa, *Panegyric*, 11.133.

6

Praying the psalms of David with Christ

SUSAN GILLINGHAM

What has catechesis to do with praying and using the psalms? A good deal, if by 'catechesis' we mean being informed about the Christian faith in such a way that we can live out that faith with confidence and integrity. First, the psalms have always been understood as a 'little Bible', containing much Old Testament thought in their prayers and teaching, and next to the Gospels, they have been an important resource for Christians in helping them to understand the roots of Christian faith. Secondly, much of what we are focusing on by way of catechesis – the Beatitudes, the Ten Commandments, the Lord's Prayer, the Apostles' Creed – borrow their language from the Book of Psalms. The Psalter even opens with a Beatitude: 'Blessed are those who . . .' (Psalm 1.1). Most of the Ten Commandments are there, as well: read Psalm 15 and see how many you can find. The Psalter also contains several phrases found in the Lord's Prayer, whether it is about praising God as our King and Father or about making our requests known to him in prayer. As for the Apostles' Creed, the phrase 'seated at the right hand of the Father', for example, is a direct quotation from Psalm 110.

In order to respond to the challenge of learning through catechesis, our hearts and minds need first to be warmed by the love of God, and there is no better place to start this exercise than through the psalms. So what follows is in part teaching, and in part a motivation for prayer.

I offer here a panoramic view of the whole Book of Psalms. Although I have no real issue with believers who pick up just one verse from a psalm here and there (indeed, our liturgy does this all the time), it is also important to 'stand back' and get a sense of the bigger picture of what the whole Psalter is about. This can provide a favourite verse or favourite psalm with more breadth and depth. And as I encourage you to look at the Book of Psalms as a whole, I also encourage you to start not with Jesus, but with David, because Jesus the Jew would have prayed the psalms of David and it's important we learn from his example.

The psalms tell a story. To know the storylines in the Bible is an important part of catechesis. We can do this through reading a Gospel, or through reading the Book of Acts; we can do it through reading parts of Genesis and Exodus as well, which are of course the beginnings of the Jewish story of salvation. But we can also do this through becoming familiar with the story of the psalms. It is, in the first instance, a story about David and the People of Israel; it is, secondly, a story about Jesus and the Church.

Reading and praying the psalms as an entire book was in fact an early Jewish practice. It soon became a Christian practice as well. As early as the end of the second century Hippolytus of Rome argued, in his sermons on the psalms, that churches ought to pray through the Psalter *as a whole*, rather than using individual psalms here and there. By the third century, monks in the desert prayed through the entire Psalter daily, and as early as the sixth century it was common monastic practice to read through the Book of Psalms every week. By the thirteenth century small books for prayer and teaching, called Prymers and Books of Hours, were produced – some with extraordinary illustrations – and along with the Creed, the Lord's Prayer and the Ten Commandments, all the psalms were often included as well. Even in the sixteenth century, the Book of Common Prayer's lectionary assumed we should read through the entire Book of Psalms every month. And although *Common Worship* provides us with particular set psalms for every day, it too has a provision for reading the whole Book of Psalms over the period of a month.

This is an introduction to the story running throughout the Book of Psalms – first the story of David and God's people, and then the story of Christ and his people, the Church.

The Psalter's story may begin with David, in roughly 1000BCE, but it is a story that ends some eight hundred years later when the Hebrew psalms were translated into Greek. The story unfolds through five smaller books of unequal lengths. (We know this because at the end of each book, at Psalms 41, 72, 89 and 106, there is a short one-verse hymn of praise that brings each book to a conclusion.) This fivefold division imitates the five books of Moses – from Genesis to Deuteronomy – at the beginning of the Old Testament. This reveals something important about the place of the Psalms of David alongside the Laws of Moses.

The five Books of Psalms are shown in Figure 1, which is a guide for what follows. The characterizations (e.g. Korah, Aspah, Hallel) will be explained below.

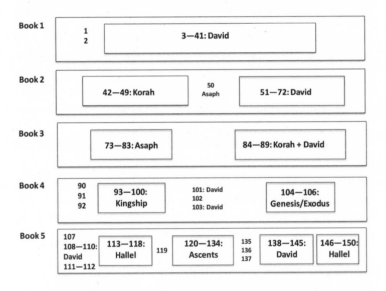

The story of David and the people of God

Book One

The first book (up to Psalm 41) is prefaced by Psalms 1 and 2, which act as a prologue to the Psalter, telling us what the key themes of the story are. Because of this, neither has that frequent heading 'Psalm of David'.

Psalm 1 starts with a Beatitude, and continues to speak about the importance of praying the Torah: 'their delight is in the law of the LORD, and on his law they meditate day and night' (Psalm 1.2). Psalm 2 is about God's special love for the king as a descendant of the line of David: '"I have set my king on Zion, my holy hill." . . . I will tell of the decree of the LORD: He said to me, "You are my son; today I have begotten you"' (Psalm 2.6–7). So, as these introductory psalms make clear, the story of the Book of Psalms revolves around two key themes – about prayer and obedience to the Law of Moses, and about God's choice of David who is the 'anointed one', or the Messiah. It is already clear why Christians saw Jesus so clearly in the psalms – he is the second Moses, bringing in the new teaching, for example in the Sermon on the Mount, and he is the second David, born of the Davidic line and showing us that royal authority is as much about suffering and dying as about exercising military power.

Book One of the Psalter therefore really consists of Psalms 3—41. It divides into four smaller collections of 12 psalms, ten psalms, another ten psalms, and seven psalms. The heading 'Psalm of David' is over every single psalm except two. As Bishop Steven has written in his doctoral thesis and in his book *The Identity of the Individual in the Book of Psalms*, the heading 'Psalm of David' does not mean authorship but is rather a way of using David as a model of piety. We agree that the 'I' might sometimes be a king, sometimes be an unknown individual, and sometimes a liturgical official, such as a prophet, a scribe, or a Temple singer. So the title 'Psalm of David' is not to be read as biographical, but rather a means of giving the psalm authority through David as a royal figure of antiquity. We are to pray these psalms, therefore *through* David.

Almost all the psalms in Book One are laments or complaints to God about the evil and suffering in the world and they often include a resolution about trust in God. It is significant that at the centre of each of these four collections is a very different psalm – a hymn of praise to God as Creator.

The first collection runs from Psalms 3 to 14. At the heart of it is Psalm 8, which praises God as Creator of the night sky: 'When I look at your heavens, the work of your fingers, the moon and the stars that you have established; what are human beings that you are mindful of them, mortals that you care for them?' The second collection is of Psalms 15 to 24. At its centre is Psalm 19, which praises God as Creator of the sun: 'in the heavens he has set a tent for the sun, which comes out like a bridegroom from his wedding canopy, and like a strong man runs its course with joy.' The third collection comprises Psalms 25 to 34. Psalm 29 is in the middle, and this psalm praises God as the one who brings about the thunder and lightnings of the storm: 'The voice of the LORD is over the waters; the God of glory thunders, the LORD, over mighty waters.' And in the fourth collection, containing Psalms 35 to 41, Psalm 38 lies at the heart, praising God for creating all human life.

So Book One, Psalms 3—41, might be compared to a piece of music, where the darkness of the pain, expressed through laments and dissonant rhythms and notes, is offset by these four celebratory hymns of praise about the power and constancy of God as Creator. For the Jewish people, from the time of David onwards, constantly facing the challenges of polytheism, this was a powerful reminder that there is *one* Creator God, who is also a personal and loving God and listens to the prayers of David and to those who pray like him.

Book Two

In Book Two we find a different heading for the first group of psalms. These are no longer called 'Psalms of David'. Each of Psalms 42—49 has a heading 'Psalms of Korah'. (Only Psalm 43, attached to Psalm 42 by a refrain, lacks this superscription.) Mostly they speak of a longing for the presence of God in an unjust world, and mostly they yearn for God's presence at the Temple in Jerusalem. Take Psalm 42 for example: 'As a deer longs for flowing streams, so my soul longs for you,

O God. My soul thirsts for God, for the living God. When shall I come and behold the face of God?'

This collection was probably preserved by Temple singers belonging to guild called Korah: some of the headings also refer to their musical use, such as 'a song'.

The other large collection in Book Two (Psalms 51—72) comprises more 'Psalms of David'. But mostly they use a different name for God than in Psalms 3—41, and their headings have many extra details, not used at all in Book One, about the problems David encountered with Saul before he succeeded him as king. So here we see that God does not give his chosen ones an easy time; nevertheless, he hears their prayer. As with Book One, we pray these psalms 'through' David, seeing him as a model of obedience and prayer. The additional musical instructions in the headings show how these psalms were later used for singing at the Temple: here the more private and personal prayers come into the public domain, rather like some of our Christmas and Easter hymns today.

This collection offers us another compact story of David. Psalm 51 starts with a lament which reminds us of David's adulterous relationship with Bathsheba: 'Have mercy on me, O God, according to your steadfast love; according to your abundant mercy blot out my transgressions. Wash me thoroughly from my iniquity, and cleanse me from my sin.' Psalm 72, the final psalm, is about the rise of King Solomon, David's son: 'Of Solomon. Give the king your justice, O God, and your righteousness to a king's son. May he judge your people with righteousness, and your poor with justice.' Solomon was actually Bathsheba's second son, so this is a reminder that God can bring good things even out of the disobedience of Israel's king.

Book Three

You might have noticed an isolated Psalm 50 in Book Two, with the heading 'Asaph'. It acts as a preface to the second Davidic Psalter; its views on the importance of integrity of prayer within ritual and sacrifice are very similar to the prayer ascribed to David about Bathsheba in Psalm 51. It speaks about offering God 'a sacrifice of thanksgiving' from the heart.

Here in Book Three there is a further collection of 11 psalms with the heading 'Psalm of Asaph', making, with Psalm 50, 12 psalms in all. These psalms have additional headings that suggest they have been compiled together, like a small hymn book, for use in Temple worship. Their tone, however, is very different from the Psalms of Korah in Book Two: instead of a more personal yearning for the presence of God, these are more communal psalms and they are acutely aware of the judgement of God on all his people. Some of them refer to northern tribes such as 'Joseph' and 'Ephraim' and suggest the influence of the northern kingdom before it fell to the Assyrians, in c. 721BCE. Psalm 80 is one example: 'Give ear, O Shepherd of Israel, you who lead Joseph like a flock! You who are enthroned upon the cherubim, shine forth before Ephraim and Benjamin and Manasseh. Stir up your might, and come to save us!' Other psalms refer to the fall of the southern kingdom and the destruction of the Temple and the exile under the Babylonians between 596 and 586BCE. Psalms 74 and 79 are obvious examples: 'O God, why do you cast us off forever? Why does your anger smoke against the sheep of your pasture? Direct your steps to the perpetual ruins; the enemy has destroyed everything in the sanctuary. Your foes have roared within your holy place; they set up their emblems there.'

In these psalms, David has all but disappeared: these are national psalms of the entire people living out despair and persecution, between two and four hundred years after the time of David, before and after the northern and then the southern kingdoms were destroyed.

Book Three ends with five other psalms whose headings are again associated with the 'sons of Korah' (84, 85, 87, 88 and 89); this makes 12 Korahite psalms in all. Like the earlier group of Korahite psalms, they are full of longing for the presence of God in the Temple, and are more personal in tone. In the heart of this collection there is one single psalm 'of David', Psalm 86:

'A Prayer of David. Incline your ear, O LORD, and answer me, for I am poor and needy.' The figure of David is also found, very clearly, in Psalm 89. This psalm is the turning point in the story of the entire Psalter. First we read of God's promises of an eternal dynasty made to King David: 'You said, "I have made a covenant with my chosen one, I have sworn to my servant David: I will establish your descendants forever, and build your throne for all generations."' Here the idea of the king as a chosen 'son' of God reminds us of Psalm 2. But at the end of Psalm 89 we read of God apparently abandoning his promises to protect David and his dynasty: 'But now you have spurned and rejected him; you are full of wrath against your anointed. You have renounced the covenant with your servant; you have defiled his crown in the dust. You have broken through all his walls; you have laid his strongholds in ruins.'

Books One to Three thus tell an important story about the rise and fall of David, with Psalm 2 speaking positively about God's relationship with the king, and Psalm 89 despairing because God seems to have broken his promises. It is not surprising that Psalm 89 was read by early Christians in the light of the crucifixion of Christ.

Book Four

Book Four is completely different in tone, and contrasts starkly with Book Three. Its first psalm actually has a heading 'Psalm of Moses': here we are reminded of a covenant God made with his people which is centuries older than that made with David. Unlike Books One to Three, the rest of Book Four has very few headings: 'Psalm of David' only occurs in the original Hebrew in Psalms 101 and 103, perhaps reminding us that God's promises to David have not been completely forgotten. The one praying in these two psalms is, like David, a figure of prayerful obedience.

The heading 'Moses' over Psalm 90, and the contents of the last two psalms, 105 and 106, about God's provision for his people during the Exodus, remind us of the time of Moses, when the people were enslaved in Egypt and in need of God's rescue. Psalms 90–92 speak about human mortality compared with the eternal God. (Isaac Watts' hymn 'O God our Help in Ages Past' is based on Psalm 90.) The mood and contents of these psalms suggests that they were written during a period when the people had lost their king, their Temple and their promised land, and as exiles now in Babylon (from 586BCE) they needed to be reminded of God's care and protection throughout their history.

And yet amidst the despair there is praise. In Book Four human finitude and vulnerability are repeatedly contrasted with the power and constancy of God. So seven psalms break up the despair and praise God as King. For example, Psalm 97.1–2: 'The LORD is king! Let the earth rejoice; let the many coastlands be glad! Clouds and thick darkness are all around him; righteousness and justice are the foundation of his throne.' One long psalm, 104, praises God as Creator of the entire world and has similarities with Genesis 1: 'Bless the LORD, O my soul. O LORD my God, you are very great. You are clothed with honour and majesty, wrapped in light as with a garment. You stretch out the heavens like a tent, you set the beams of your chambers on the waters, you make the clouds your chariot, you ride on the wings of the wind.'

Anyone who has read Isaiah 40–55, also believed to have been composed during the exilic period, will find many connections with Book Four of the Psalter, as both the prophet and the psalms frequently recall God as their Creator and their King.

Book Four overall comprises psalms of faith sung by a people whose experience of God as Creator and King was at its lowest ebb. Yet it marks the beginnings of a communal *hope* in the Books of Psalms, where faith rises above experience. God's constancy and world rule are upheld even though they seem far away when faced with Babylonian rule. That's why Psalms 96 and 98 speak of praising God with a 'new song'. At the very end of the Book we hear for the first time 'Hallelujah! Praise God.' This is a theme that is increasingly persistent in Book Five.

Book Five

In Book Five the story of the psalms reaches its conclusion. It uses the themes of the other books and weaves them into an ongoing story of hope. There are two short collections of psalms headed 'Psalms of David'. One is at the beginning (Psalms 108—110) and the other is near the end (Psalms 138—145), and these remind us that God has not forgotten his promise made to David, despite all appearances. The first Davidic collection focuses on God's vindication of the king, as seen especially in Psalm 110: 'The LORD says to my lord, "Sit at my right hand until I make your enemies your footstool." The LORD sends out from Zion your mighty sceptre. Rule in the midst of your foes.' The second Davidic collection, Psalms 138—145, takes up the theme of David as obedient and prayerful, one who is a model of righteous suffering for us to follow.

The two 'Alleluia' collections, also known as 'Hallel Psalms' from the Hebrew, are Psalms 113—118 and Psalms 146—150, and each follows a Davidic collection of psalms; they remind us that, whatever happens to God's people, God is still their King. The first Alleluia collection returns to the theme in Book Four, that God proved his Kingship by redeeming his people from slavery in Egypt. The second Alleluia collection, at the very end of the Psalter, takes up the theme of other psalms that praise God as Creator of the universe. His plan is not only for the people of David, nor only for the people of Moses, but includes the whole world. So Psalm 150 reads: 'Praise him with clanging cymbals; praise him with loud clashing cymbals! Let everything that breathes praise the LORD! Praise the LORD!'

God's plans for his people require some response. The long Torah Psalm, 119, like Psalm 1, reflects on the other part of the Exodus story, the giving of the Law to Moses on Mount Sinai. The Law is not an irksome duty, but it is a gift of grace from God. Again, like Psalm 1, we see the importance of prayer and obedience.

Smaller psalms of instruction (111 and 112) and other psalms about God's provision for his people in the face of awful suffering (135, 136 and 137) have been interwoven into this story.

Finally, at the heart of Book Five, is the large collection of 15 pilgrimage psalms, 120–134. This collection, called 'Songs of Ascents' because each psalm has that title, may well have been used when the people made their pilgrimage up to Jerusalem, perhaps at harvest time. This collection reminds the people that Jerusalem still plays an important part in God's plans for his people: the Jerusalem Temple is where they will finally receive God's blessing. For example, Psalm 125 reads: 'Those who trust in the LORD are like Mount Zion, which cannot be moved, but abides forever. As the mountains surround Jerusalem, so the LORD surrounds his people, from this time on and for evermore.' The 'Songs of Ascents' are also profoundly personal, and they have several links with the psalms headed 'Psalms of Korah': God is seen as particularly present in the Temple and the prayers of his people witness to this.

Summary

So this is the story of Psalms, as told from the perspective of David and Israel his people.

David is the model for personal piety in the first two Books, as in Psalms 3–41 and 51–72, although by the beginning of Book Two another theme, that of the Temple, begins to emerge. Book Three moves increasingly away from David and focuses more on the dreadful things that have happened later to the people as a whole, being conquered by foreign nations such as the Assyrians and the Babylonians, and here the theme is whether their God is still a just and powerful God, given that their Temple and king had been taken away. Book Three ends with a specific lament about the end of Davidic dynasty as the people were carried into exile and their king was imprisoned.

The mood changes in Books Four and Five. Book Four, with its emphasis on God as King, shows that, despite all appearances, God is indeed just and powerful, and that he has not forgotten his people. This book is for those in despair and without a homeland. Book Five focuses on the theme of restoration; many of these psalms would have been composed after the return and used for worship in the rebuilt Temple, when the people were under Persian rule from c. 538BCE onwards. The hope for a still better future runs throughout Book Five – a future where a Davidic figure still plays a part, a future where Jerusalem and its Temple play a part, a future where the promises made to Moses also play a part, and, by the end of the Psalter, a future that might even encompass believing Gentiles as well.

The story of Jesus and the Christian Church

It should be fairly clear how the story of Jesus can be read into this five-act drama. The first two books, which are more personal prayers and laments, help us understand more about how Jesus prayed the psalms, not only during his ministry but up to his death. Take the psalms from Book One, for example. Jesus' cry from the cross: 'My God, My God, why have you forsaken me?' comes from Psalm 22, and his prayer 'Into your hands I commit my spirit' comes from Psalm 31. When Jesus speaks of being hated without cause, he is referring to Psalm 35. In Psalm 37 we read 'Blessed are the meek', used also by Jesus in the Beatitudes.

We saw how the longing for God's presence in the Temple is found in the psalms at the beginning of Book Two. In the Gospels we read how worship at the Temple played an important part in Jesus' life, from his birth and early childhood when speaking with the teachers in the Temple. We read that when Jesus cleansed the Temple he spoke of zeal for God's house having consumed him; this is from Psalm 69.

Many of the psalms ascribed to David near the end of Book Three concerned the experience of hostility and persecution from friends and enemies: Jesus experienced hostility, from the

Romans, the Jews, the crowds, and even from one of his disciples, Judas. These psalms would have nurtured his own life with God.

We noted how the mood of Book Three is dark and full of a sense of impending judgement. So in the life of Jesus, as it becomes inevitable that he will die, these psalms which ask whether God is still powerful, still just, still faithful to his promises, are as relevant in the life of Jesus as they were in the life of David and Israel. Psalm 82, for example, is a key psalm in John 12 in a heated debate about who Jesus was.

Book Four, we noted, is about the people living out the Kingship of God, and remembering his past promises even in exile. This book enables us to reflect on the despair caused by the death of Jesus within the context of all he taught us about the Kingdom of God. The theme of God's Kingship and his world rule enables us to see the possibility of new life after death in his resurrection and ascension.

We saw that Book Five was about the restoration of Israel after the exile was over. And so the new Israel, the church, reads this Book of Psalms in light of the resurrection and the growing faith of the early Church. God's presence, once found so profoundly in the Temple, is now found in the person of Christ, our 'living Temple', through the presence of the Holy Spirit. We read these psalms through the risen Jesus who is both a new David, as a suffering Messiah, and a New Moses, fulfilling the law and offering us his grace as a means of keeping his commands. Thus the story of the Psalter ends with calls of praise to the Gentiles and to the entire world: we are now able to participate in the story of David and the story of Israel through the new story of Christ and his Church.

And so the psalms offer us not one story, but two: this is the story of David and Israel – a story kept alive in Jewish faith today – but it is also the story of Christ and his Church – the story we live out as Christians. Each story has its own integrity: I am not intending to say here that the one dispenses with the other: we need to acknowledge the story that is ours without denying the worth of David's story, which after all is what gives our own faith its roots and much of its meaning.

The story about Jesus and the Christian Church

Outside the Gospels, almost every New Testament book refers to the psalms as a way of understanding the life and death of Jesus. The Book of Acts and the Epistles to the Romans and to the Hebrews are especially full of references to psalms. We might ask, though, if it is right to superimpose the story of Jesus and his Church onto the story of David and Israel by using the psalms? The answer is quite surprising. In actual fact, the way that the New Testament writers read their scriptures as prophecies, to be fulfilled in Jesus, was not new: many Jews were reading the story of the psalms as prophecies looking forward for fulfilment even before Jesus was born.

The Dead Sea Scrolls, dating from about the second century BCE, and discovered in the Judean desert from 1948 onwards, give us evidence of this. Some of the scrolls have several expansive commentaries on different collections of verses from the Hebrew Bible in order to draw up a plan for the restoration of the Temple and the part of their community within it. Members of the community read many verses in the Hebrew Bible as prophecies being fulfilled in their own day, and they selected verses from the psalms and the prophets to show that they could expect a coming figure of the branch of David, who would also be the interpreter of their law. For example, in a scroll called 11QMelchizedek, they creatively used parts of Psalms 7 and 82 to describe the redemption to be brought about by a heavenly priestly figure they called Melchizedek.

So when the New Testament Jewish Christians also used the psalms as *prophecies*, they were not being totally innovative, except that in this case they read the prophecies as referring not to a future figure, but to one who had already been born, and lived and died in Palestine: the psalms were now not about a coming figure, but about Jesus and the arrival of the Kingdom of God. The psalms were a most important resource for their interpretation of who Jesus was. Over one third of the some 360 Old Testament quotations in the New Testament come from the psalms. So in Christian thinking, the story of Jesus Christ really needed to be read in the light of David's story. The psalms might have been understood as 'by' David, but they are now 'about' Jesus Christ, and so they illustrate how the words of prayer and teaching have been fulfilled in his life, death, resurrection, ascension and in the gift of the Holy Spirit in forming the early Church.

For example, when Psalm 2.7 is quoted in Matthew, Mark and Luke ('I will tell of the decree of the Lord: He said to me, "You are my son; today I have begotten you"') this now applies specifically to Jesus. 'This is my beloved Son in whom I am well pleased' is used both at Jesus' baptism and at his transfiguration to show that God affirms Jesus, son of David, as his begotten son. When in Psalm 22 we read about the psalmist being mocked and jeered, and about his garments being given away by casting lots, the New Testament writers saw this as a prophecy about the suffering of Christ on the cross. Similarly in Psalm 69, when the psalmist speaks about being given vinegar to drink, this is read as a prophecy about Jesus' thirst when dying on the cross. And when Psalm 72 speaks about kings from the East coming to pay tribute to the King of God's People, this is now read as a prophecy about the visit to the baby Jesus from the three kings.

So how do we read and pray the psalms?

As Christians we need to know how to live out our faith in the here and now. Both the story in the psalms about David and the people of Israel and the story in the psalms about Christ and the Church are our stories too: they give us a wider perspective over space and time, and they show us how to appropriate these stories as part of our story in the 'here and now'. We need to embrace these two stories in the Psalter for ourselves: we cannot be disciples without prayer and teaching, and the Psalter shows us how to both pray and live in the light of the

God of the whole Bible. As we move through the story, psalm by psalm, there are perhaps four stages we can work through to use the psalms as part of our own story as well.

1   *A Psalm of David.* The first stage is to read a chosen psalm as an ancient prayer – i.e. a prayer ascribed to David and a prayer used by the people of Israel. These people lived in very different times from us, and this approach can often help us to understand the things we find difficult in the psalms – about the overly negative attitude to enemies, and the overly positive attitude to material rewards, for example. The psalms come from a different time and a different country: we have to respect them for what they are. So the first stage is praying the psalms as prayers of David and Israel, and allowing ourselves to absorb these different ways of thinking in our own prayers.

2   *A Psalm of Christ.* This stage is to read a psalm as a prayer that Jesus would have prayed, and so reflecting on it imaginatively through what we know of the life of Christ in the Gospels. This is where Christ in the psalms accompanies us at a most profound level on our own Christian journey: he becomes not only our example and our teacher, but the one who by coming alongside us can transform our prayers: he has been this way as well, and in understanding both the joys and sorrows of the psalmists, he can mediate the psalms to us, as his human life intersects with ours.

3   *A Psalm about Christ.* The third stage has a different focus. Here we read the psalm not as a prayer *of* David or *of* Christ, but as a prayer *about* Christ. This is something the Church has practised through the ages: we have seen how this took place in the New Testament, but it was also the way the early Church fathers often read the psalms, and this practice continued through to medieval writers, to Reformation commentators and so up to the present day. We immerse ourselves in 2000 years of history when we take this approach: we can access online many Christian commentators to help us on our journey if we find this helpful. In brief, we have to

see what the psalm teaches us *about* Christ in his human life, and what it teaches us *about* Christ as God.

4 *A Psalm addressed to Christ.* This final stage is where we turn our attention to Christ himself, bringing to this all we have thought about and prayed about before. So now we pray *to* him, rather than *with* him or *about* him. Some of the best psalms to start with are those that praise God as Creator (for example Psalms 8, 19, 29, 38 and 104) and those that praise God as King (for example Psalms 93 – 100). Here we consider Christ as the pre-existent Word who, along with the Spirit of God, brought the universe into being; and here we consider Christ, risen and ascended, who 'sits at the right hand of God' and with the Spirit of God reigns over time and into eternity. To address Christ as God is to begin to pray in the mystery of the Trinity; and to pray in the mystery of the Trinity, using the words of a psalm as we do so, is, in my own view, the highest and even the most mystical kind of prayer.

So, to conclude: catechesis is a way of helping us to know about God, and about the stories of God and his people expressed in the Bible and reflected upon in the Church. It is knowledge as 'understanding'. Catechesis through prayer, meditating and reflecting on the stories of God and his people throughout the Bible, is a way of helping us to move from *knowing about God* with our minds to *knowing God* with our hearts. In this sense catechesis is not only about 'understanding' the Christian faith but also about 'encountering' God in Christ, and indeed about encountering God as Trinity as noted above. In brief, catechesis is about both the mind and the heart. We cannot have one without the other. Of all the books in the Bible the Psalter is paramount in enabling us to read and pray not only with our minds but also with our hearts, and so in my view it stands at the centre of what catechesis is all about.

7

'Approaching the stony and barren hearts of the pagans': The place of catechesis in the Anglo-Saxon missions

SARAH FOOT

In the year 723 or 724, Daniel Bishop of Winchester wrote a letter to one of his former diocesan clergy, who was evangelizing in Hesse and Thuringia. Originally called Winfrith, this priest had recently obtained a papal commission to preach to the heathen east of the Rhine and assumed the name Boniface. Bishop Daniel expressed delight at the virtue displayed by Boniface in undertaking the task of evangelism:

> You have approached the hitherto stony and barren hearts of the pagans, trusting in the plenitude of your faith, and have laboured untiringly with the ploughshare of Gospel preaching, striving by your daily toil to change them into fertile fields. To you may well be applied the Gospel saying 'the voice of one crying in the wilderness etc.'[1]

The bishop was optimistic that divine favour would fall on those who 'support so pious and useful a work with what help they can give and supplement the poverty of those labourers with means sufficient to carry on zealously the work of preaching that has already been begun and to raise up new sons to Christ.' With that in mind, the bishop sought to advise Boniface on how to approach the task of mission, so that he might 'most readily overcome the resistance of these "uncivilized" people'.

Since it deals directly with missionary methods (specifically with means by which to counter polytheism), Bishop Daniel's letter provides a useful introduction to the ways in which early medieval church leaders approached the problem of initial instruction in the Christian faith. The bishop's advice focused on the benefits of overcoming the resistance of pagans by countering their belief in multiple gods. Crucial to that argument, to the bishop's mind, was the fact that such gods had a beginning; one can describe how they were created and begotten. But what about the world itself, he asked: 'if the world had a beginning who created it?' His arguments about the origins of man-made gods, and the inefficacy of their actions, led him naturally to reflect on the one God who created heaven and earth. 'Show them', he argued, 'that the whole world was once given over to idol-worship, until by the grace of Christ and through the knowledge of one God, its Almighty Founder and Ruler, it was enlightened, brought to life and reconciled to God. For what is the daily baptism of the children of believing Christians but purification of each one from the uncleanness and guilt in which the whole world was once involved?'[2] This letter provides a useful summary of the key issues relating to catechesis in an early medieval Germanic context.

But what was an Anglo-Saxon priest and monk doing in the German mission-field when the conversion of the last English kingdom had been effected only one generation previously? We need to set Boniface's evangelizing work in a longer historical context, touching on the ways that his own nation came to faith.

The apostles' faithful adherence to Christ's final injunction to his disciples on the Mount of Olives before his Ascension led to the spread of the faith far beyond Jerusalem towards the ends of the earth. As Christianity spread through the Roman Empire, so it came to Roman Britain, where we know of the existence of Christians at least by the year 314, when some British bishops attended a Council in Arles. By then there must have been a network of churches and some diocesan structure, seemingly with centres at London and at York as well as in other Roman cities. But after the departure of Roman troops in 409, as pagan Germanic peoples from the European mainland came to British shores and began to settle in significant numbers, the surviving Christian population seems to have dwindled in size, the largest remaining concentrations of believers being found in the west of the island. Some practising Christians remained in areas of dense Anglo-Saxon settlement, for example at Verulamium which had the shrine of early Christian martyr St Alban (d. c. AD 303). In the 590s there was also in the city of Canterbury at least one church, dedicated to the Gallic missionary bishop, St Martin. Yet Christianity was largely unknown across much of England and Scotland by the end of the sixth century.[3]

Within a century, however, every separate kingdom of Anglo-Saxon England had, at least nominally, been brought within the fold of western Christendom, thanks to the work of different groups of missionaries who came from Rome, Ireland (via the Scottish island monastery of Iona) and from Frankia to preach the gospel. A range of factors must have contributed to the remarkable success of these missionary endeavours. This essay asks how important a role catechesis played in explaining that achievement. It will explore what we know about the early missions, concentrating on the Roman missionaries whose activities are recorded most fully; then it will consider how clergy taught the fundamentals of the Christian faith to a partially-Christianized population; and finally it will return to the English missions in continental Europe in the eighth century in which Boniface played a central role.

The conversion of the English kingdoms

Much of our information about the first mission to the pagan Anglo-Saxons, that sent from Rome by Gregory the Great to Kent in 597, comes from the pages of the *Ecclesiastical History of the English People*, written by the Venerable Bede in the late 720s. So long after the events of the initial conversion, Bede often had only remembered traditions about how individual priests had taught the faith on which to draw. He did, however, support his narrative with the texts of a number of letters written by Pope Gregory and his successors to kings, queens and senior clergy in Gaul and England, encouraging them to support the missionaries and their endeavours; those texts give some insight into how the task of basic Christian teaching was understood in this period.

Gregory sent monks from his own monastery in Rome to preach the word to the English, establishing a link between mission and monasticism that would have enduring significance for the shape of the early English Church. Although the group set off obediently enough, they had not gone far on their journey before they became 'paralysed with terror. They began to contemplate returning home rather than going to a barbarous, fierce and unbelieving nation whose language they did not even understand.' Augustine, their leader, went back to Rome to ask Gregory if they might be released from his charge, but the pope firmly set them back on track, urging them not to let 'the toilsome journey nor the tongues of evil speakers' deter them, but to hold fast to the eternal reward that would await them. He thought also of their practical needs and arranged that Gaulish interpreters accompany the Roman monks to England, since they would be able to talk to the pagan English in their own tongue.[4] The theme of translation – both of the language of Christianity, a religion of the book, and of the cultural practices of the new religion – is one that we will encounter again.

When the party arrived on the island of Thanet, off the eastern tip of Kent, Augustine sent a message to the local king (Æthelberht) to say 'that he had come from Rome bearing the best of news, namely the sure and certain promise of eternal joys in heaven, and an endless kingdom with the living and true God to those who received it'.[5] Beyond this statement, Bede had nothing to say about how Augustine and his companions sought to catechize the king – who had already had some exposure to the faith because his Frankish wife was a

Christian – or his leading men. He dwelt more on the example that Augustine's companions presented of Christian living (singing psalms and hymns, reciting litanies, going in procession, engaging in prayers, vigils and fasts), and 'preaching'. But what they preached, Bede does not say. Whatever catechetical methods they used, Augustine and his companions were remarkably successful, for Gregory boasted to Eulogius, Patriarch of Alexandria, that at Christmas that first year, more than ten thousand of the English had been baptized by the newly-consecrated bishop.[6] The first missionaries' anxieties about the likely behaviour of 'this fierce and unbelieving nation' had seemingly proved unfounded.

Papal correspondence offers some insights about how the missionaries approached the practical problems they encountered among the pagan English. One key question over which Pope Gregory proved, perhaps surprisingly, rather inconsistent was that of how to treat former pagan places of worship. Initially, he told Æthelberht to suppress the worship of idols, and overthrow their buildings and shrines.[7] But later he changed his mind, deciding that the temples should not be destroyed, only the idols in them. He advised that they be cleansed with holy water and altars with relics placed within them. 'For if the shrines are well built, it is essential that they should be changed from the worship of devils to the service of the true God. When the people see that their shrines are not destroyed, they will be able to banish error from their hearts and be more ready to come to the places with which they are familiar, but now recognizing and worshipping the true God.'[8] Gregory's letters indicate how much the issue of pagan gods and their worship preoccupied those engaged in mission among Germanic pagans.

In his account of the Roman mission to Northumbria led by one of the second-generation missionaries, Paulinus, Bede provided a lengthier narrative of the process by which the king came to faith. Over four consecutive chapters, Bede explained how and why the Northumbrian king, and with him his leading men, decided to turn away from the gods of his forefathers and towards the one true God. Edwin, the pagan king of the Northumbrians, had married the Christian daughter of Æthelberht of Kent, Æthelburh, but he refused to accept the faith that his wife professed unless he could bring his leading men to baptism with him. Paulinus (who had accompanied Æthelburh to Northumbria) worked vigorously among Edwin's people, trying to convert them to grace and faith.[9] An unsuccessful assassination attempt, the safe birth of a daughter (and her baptism at Pentecost), together with a victory over his enemies, all helped to sway Edwin's mind and turn him from the worship of idols. Even so, he still hesitated over accepting the Christian faith, seeking further teaching from Paulinus and the advice of his leading men.

The then pope, Boniface, tried to alter the king's mind by providing catechetical instruction in writing, addressing letters to both Edwin and to his wife, Æthelburh. In writing to Edwin, Boniface dwelt particularly on God as Creator of world – 'heaven and earth, the sea and all that is in them' – and of the making of man in God's own image. But he paid almost as much attention to the wrongness of belief in pagan gods and idols, quoting words from the psalms to demonstrate the limitations of man-made idols, and urging the king to abandon the devil and all his works and turn to God, the indivisible Trinity, in words that deliberately echoed the liturgy of the baptismal service.[10] Clearly the polytheism of the Anglo-Saxons preoccupied and concerned the pope considerably. Similarly, in his letter to Edwin's wife, Pope Boniface expressed his regret that her husband still served idols. He worried that their marital union risked corruption through Edwin's refusal to commit to the Christian God and urged Æthelburh to bring her husband to faith. He advised her to explain the greatness of the mystery of belief, and to inflame his cold heart by teaching him about the Holy Spirit: 'Then the testimony of holy scripture will be clearly and abundantly fulfilled in you: "The unbelieving husband shall be saved by the believing wife."'[11]

Pride constituted a significant impediment to the conversion of the king, who had difficulty turning humbly to the way of salvation and accepting the mystery of the life-giving cross. A key factor in persuading him to a change of heart came in the form of the fulfilment of a previous vision, and Paulinus' patient (but largely undescribed) teaching, which dwelt on both the earthly rewards and achievements that Edwin already enjoyed, while pointing to the fact that acceptance of faith would 'rescue him from the everlasting torments of the wicked and make Edwin a partaker with God in his eternal kingdom in heaven'.[12] Just how influential the promise of eternal life would prove became clear at the climax of Bede's narrative about Northumbria's conversion: the moment when the king gathered his leading counsellors to discuss the new faith. At this meeting, an unknown thegn uttered what is perhaps the most famous passage of reported speech from the entire Anglo-Saxon period:

This is how the present life of man on earth, King, appears to me in comparison with that time which is unknown to us. You are sitting feasting with your ealdormen and thegns in winter time; the fire is burning on the hearth in the middle of the hall and all inside is warm, while outside the wintry storms of rain and snow are raging; and a sparrow flies swiftly through the hall. It enters in at one door and quickly flies out through the other. For a few moments it is inside, the storm and wintry tempest cannot touch it, but after the briefest moment of calm, it flits from your sight, out of the wintry storm and into it again. So the life of man appears but for a moment; what follows, or indeed what went before, we know not at all. If this new doctrine brings us more certain information, it seems right that we should accept it.[13]

We might wonder how a pagan thegn could so have absorbed the teaching of Paulinus that in articulating his own uncertainty about the afterlife, he proved able to allude both to Psalm 84 and to the Gospel of Matthew (10.29–31). And we might hesitate about the actions attributed to the chief priest of the pagans, Coifi (whose name may bring to mind the High

Priest Caiaphas: see Julia Barrow, 'How Coifi pierced Christ's side'). Yet, however much we recognize Bede's artifice in this account, we should note his emphasis on the fate of the soul after death, reflecting Bede's own understanding of the issues that would most have preoccupied those hesitating on the brink of conversion. In the context of Edwin's imagined council, Bede contrived to show how God's grace worked through a range of different agents and in various ways to bring salvation to Northumbrians. Telling that overarching story – part of the longer narrative of the spreading of the gospel away from Jerusalem to the ends of the earth – was significantly more important to Bede than descriptions of the precise means by which the missionaries provided catechetical teaching.

Despite a number of setbacks along the way, the evangelization of the English proved so successful that by the end of the seventh century every Anglo-Saxon kingdom had nominally turned towards Christ. The last people to come to faith were the South Saxons, whom Wilfrid, bishop of Northumbria, evangelized, in Bede's words rescuing them 'not only from the misery of everlasting damnation, but also from temporal death and cruel destruction'. For Wilfrid arrived in the region during a period of acute famine in which many had died, but 'on the very day on which the people of Sussex received the baptism of faith' it began to rain, the earth revived and a fruitful season of plenty followed. So, all the people began to rejoice in the living God for having endowed them with both outward and inward blessings.[14]

In each of these accounts of the English conversion, Bede recounted a similar, top-down narrative in which missionaries approached first the ruler of a given region and sought to convert him and his immediate circle before proceeding to evangelize the wider population. Access to kings was obviously crucial to a mission's success, for they played the central role in determining which god (or gods) their subjects would worship. One factor that may surprise us as we read these accounts: not one of these evangelists died in order to bring the English to faith. No martyrs are associated with either the first Roman mission, nor the later missions sent from Iona or Frankia. Yet, as already observed, the first Roman missionaries expected to die at the hands of the 'barbarous, fierce and unbelieving nation' to which Gregory sent them. Even though their fears proved unfounded during the initial stages of the mission, their successors discovered that after the first Christian kings had died, their sons' decisions to reinstate the old faith put Christian clergy (and indeed some members of the old king's family) at considerable risk.

After the death of the first Christian king of Essex, his sons began to practise idolatry and allowed their subjects to worship idols. Refused access to the Eucharist by Mellitus unless that they accepted baptism, the heathen young men, enraged, expelled the bishop and his companions from Essex.[15] Together with his fellow bishops, Justus and Laurence in Kent, Mellitus determined to return to his own country, rather than to 'remain fruitlessly among these barbarians who had rebelled against the faith'; he and Justus (bishop of Rochester) thus departed forthwith for Gaul. But Laurence, archbishop of Canterbury who would have followed, changed his mind after a night-time visitation from St Peter, who scourged him and castigated him for planning to desert the flock entrusted to him. Showing his wounds to the Kentish king and reporting the apostle's teaching, the archbishop persuaded him to abandon his idolatrous worship, accept baptism and promote the interests of the church in his realm. Mellitus and Justus were recalled from Gaul, and Justus readily resumed his seat in Rochester; it took rather longer for the people of London to turn to God and accept Mellitus' ministry.[16]

Similarly, the kingdom of Northumbria was thrown into confusion after the death of Edwin, and Paulinus fled back to Kent with Æthelburh, Edwin's queen, and their children while the new kings in Northumbria 'abjured and betrayed the mysteries of the heavenly kingdom to which they had been admitted and reverted to the filth of their former idolatry'.[17] Flight may have appeared the only recourse for the bishop and the only way to ensure the safety of the Christian members of the royal family, but we must wonder whether the danger were as severe as Paulinus assumed. For James the Deacon ('a true churchman and a saintly man') remained in the church of York after Paulinus' flight and continued to teach and baptize, rescuing many in the region from the errors of paganism and promoting the faith, especially singing in the church once Christianity was restored to the kingdom.[18]

Why were none of the early missionaries in fact martyred for their faith? For all their anxiety about the dangers they faced, no one appears to have come to harm. Various possible reasons present themselves but we might wonder how influential were the missionaries' catechetical methods. If they dwelt on the positive benefits of believing (and on the promises of eternal life that Christianity offers), without focusing unduly on sins unwittingly committed by the pagans before they knew of the one true God, perhaps they did not represent a sufficient threat to the Anglo-Saxons' sense of their own distinctive cultural identity to put themselves in danger of suffering harm. This would not prove to be the case when the English started to evangelize in foreign mission fields, however.

The earliest Anglo-Saxon mission in Europe

Soon after the conversion of the South Saxons to the faith, individual English Christians began to feel sufficiently confident about their own faith and the completion of the initial work of mission among their compatriots to turn their evangelizing attention and energies overseas. From the 690s onwards, English missionaries began to work in the Rhineland, converting unbelievers to the faith and restoring to orthodox practice groups of people who had previously had some encounters with Christianity, but had reverted towards their former superstitious practices because of a lack of continuing pastoral care and support to keep them secure in their new faith.

One of the first to engage in foreign mission was Bishop Wilfrid, who encountered heathen people among the Frisians while on a visit to Rome in 678/9. Encouraged by their king, Aldgisl, Wilfrid spent a period of time there preaching and teaching about the triune God and the value of baptism for the remission of sins. While Wilfrid's endeavours bore some immediate fruit, bringing benefits that the former pagans recognized through the fruitfulness of their land and an abundant catch of fish,[19] its enduring significance lay less in his success in converting some unbelievers as in the fact that he opened the eyes of his compatriots to the possibility of mission in continental Europe. The generation of Northumbrians who travelled to Frisia and Germany after him believed that Wilfrid had laid the foundations on which his pupil, Willibrord, would come to build a permanent church in Frisia. Indeed, by the time that Wilfrid travelled again to Rome in 703 he could stay with Willibrord on his journey. Within another twenty years, as the political situation in Frisia stabilized following the secure expansion of Frankish power eastwards, other English missionaries began to evangelize east of the Rhine. Among them was the young man from Devon called Winfrith, who would take the name of a late Roman martyr, Boniface, as his name in religion. We should not, however, forget the continuing labours undertaken after the initial Christianization of each English kingdom to embed a fuller understanding of the gospel message among the wider native population through catechesis.

Catechesis and pastoral care

In comparison with the dramatic narratives that Bede couched to describe the initial conversion of different groups of Anglo-Saxon people, his accounts of how clerics continued to impart the fundamentals of the Christian faith thereafter are more low-key. While Bede frequently mentioned the labours of prominent clergy who travelled to minister to rural populations, he seldom said much about the nature of the teaching in which they engaged. For pastors such as Cuthbert or John of Beverley, who often ventured out into remote villages where the people would gather round them to hear their teaching, and receive baptism, translation played a key role. Not only did clergy have to explain in the vernacular the teachings of a gospel that they could read in Latin, but they had also to explain the rituals and sacraments of Christianity in ways that made them comprehensible to a people brought up in a wholly different sort of religious experience. The ministry of these men (and indeed religious women, who also engaged directly in the Christian education of their lay neighbours) closely followed scriptural models. All shared the ambition to be Christ-like in ministry, to search out those of the flock who had strayed or were lost, to be with new believers in their first tentative steps of faith and to walk alongside those who already had some confidence in the gospel. Yet in Bede's mind, Cuthbert encapsulated the fulfilment of those precepts most fully; his was a model ministry, combining the ascetic rigours of his solitary life with active engagement as a pastor. Although we know that on his trips away from Lindisfarne he often ended up baptizing new believers, we know no details about what he taught. Presumably, he focused on the central elements of faith, starting with the Lord's Prayer and the Creed before perhaps turning to the Ten Commandments and the Beatitudes.

In a strongly-worded letter that he addressed to his diocesan bishop, Ecgberht of York, in 734, Bede wrote eloquently about the need for priests to be 'ordained and teachers established who may preach the word of God and consecrate the holy mysteries in every small village, and above all perform the holy rites of baptism wherever the opportunity arises'. In that work he thought it crucial to teach the beliefs of the Church as encapsulated in the Apostles' Creed, and also the Lord's Prayer. Acknowledging that those who had good Latin would know these texts well, Bede advised that others, both lay people and clergy, should learn to say them 'in their own tongue and to chant them carefully'. To this end, Bede noted that he had frequently offered an English translation of the Creed and the Lord's Prayer to uneducated priests. This passing comment sheds interesting light on the levels of Latinity attained by the clergy of Bede's own day. It also indicates how much his own understanding of catechesis rested on the use of the Creed and the Lord's Prayer as the essential tools of Christian education, casting interesting light on the use of the vernacular in that task.

It may be that at least part of the ceremony of baptism was performed in the vernacular. An English church council from the year 747 stipulated that those who brought infants to the font ought to learn in English those parts of the liturgy in which they had an active role to play, namely the renunciation of the devil and the profession of faith. Officiating clergy must have been accustomed to explain in the vernacular the meaning of the words that that they would go on to say in Latin. The evidence of the Old Saxon, or Utrecht, baptismal promise (a text that survives only from the context of the mission-field in Saxony but may have been Anglo-Saxon in origin) demonstrates that portions of the rite itself were said in Old Saxon. The priest asked candidates in the vernacular to renounce the devil, all pagan sacrifices, and 'all the devil's works and words; Thunar and Woden and Saxnot and all the demons that are their companions', before making their confession of faith in God the Father, Son and Holy Spirit.[20] It can be no coincidence that of all the elements of the baptismal liturgy it is the renunciation of the devil and the profession of faith that have survived in a vernacular form. Interrogation about intention lies at the heart of the rite, for the baptizand had to declare publicly their understanding of what they were giving up of their old life and to what it was that they now sought to commit themselves.[21]

Whether working among unconverted pagans (in England or in Frisia and Germany) or with a population that had already received some Christian teaching, all clergy and pastoral workers clearly encountered enduring pagan practices and superstitions among their flock. Some insight into the difficulties that these presented comes from the Penitential attributed to the late seventh-century English archbishop, Theodore, who made a number of recommendations about how clergy should handle those who for example continued to worship idols, performed incantations or divinations, or who ate food sacrificed to pagan gods.[22] He legislated against interfaith marriages between Christians and unbelievers,[23] and addressed the problem of pagan burials in churches, for recent converts apparently wanted to have ancestors buried in consecrated churches, or to build churches over their graves. Theodore took a hard line, prescribing that altars must not be consecrated in places where the bodies of unbelievers were buried.[24] Theodore's recommendations, like Gregory's responses to Augustine's questions in the early days of the mission, all focus directly on the practical issues that arose out of trying to teach the essentials of the Christian faith in cultural contexts to which they were alien.

Unsuccessful missions

For all the triumphs of the early missions to which Bede bore witness in his *History* we should recall that not all efforts at evangelization met with equal success. An Irish monk called Dícuill established a small monastery in Sussex with a few companions and preached to the locals, but the natives did not want to follow their way of life, nor listen to their teaching.[25] More dramatically, a Frankish missionary, Wulfram, attempted to convert the pagan king of the Frisians, Radbod. The king hesitated as he stepped into the font, worrying about 'where the greater part of the kings, princes, and nobles of the Frisian people were: in the celestial realm that Wulfram had promised him to be shown if he believed and would be baptized, or in that region that he called the Tartarus of damnation?' Once the bishop confirmed that only those who believe and are baptized can enjoy eternal bliss, Radbod withdrew his foot from the font preferring to join the company of his predecessors, the princes of the Frisians, rather than residing with a small number of the poor in the celestial kingdom.[26] This episode demonstrates how important the problem of the automatic condemnation of pagan forebears was in these Germanic cultures in which a family's ancestors played a significant role in its conception of its own identity. It may be, however, that as the story has survived to us, it reveals less about missionary methods in Radbod's day than about problems that Boniface and others encountered in the 740s over how to handle the question of unbaptized forebears; Boniface took a particularly hard line over this question, but an Irish bishop called Clemens, who was active in eastern Frankia, appears to have been more generous in his interpretation of the likely fate of the unbaptized.[27]

We encounter another example of the difficulties of cultural translation in the story of the two English brothers both called Hewald, who evangelized among the Saxons to the east of the Rhine, without enjoying the protection of the local rulers. When the barbarians saw the brothers continually engaged in psalmody and prayer and in offering the sacrifice of the mass on a portable altar, they realized that these were men of a different religion. As Bede explained, they consequently began to suspect that, if the Hewalds came to their leader and talked to him, 'they might turn him away from their gods and bring him to a new faith, the Christian religion, and so gradually the whole land would be compelled to change its old religion for a new one. So they seized them suddenly and put them to death.'[28] Once again, we see how the new faith might threaten the underpinnings of a Germanic society; the Saxons' sense of their own distinctive identity was closely linked to their pagan religious practices.

Against this background, we now have a much clearer sense of the contexts in which Boniface found himself as he tried to bring the good news of salvation to pagans in Frisia, Saxony and other German lands. He showed a keen awareness of the need to create a formal ecclesiastical infrastructure in the places where he had evangelized, learning from the example of his predecessors that the new faith could not be embedded among the population without the establishment of churches staffed with clergy to provide pastoral care and teaching to the newly baptized. Some of his letters provide insights into the difficulties he encountered on the ground, particularly over ensuring that baptism had been properly administered. One letter of Pope Gregory's includes a recommendation that Boniface should rebaptize in the name of the Trinity those who had received baptism from 'pagans', as well as any who were uncertain as to whether they had received baptism. Those baptized by priests who sacrificed to Jupiter or who participated in pagan sacrificial meals should also undergo another baptism. These papal demands raise a number of questions about the identity of these pagans apparently baptizing heathens and the confusion their activities created among genuine believers who found themselves uncertain about their own baptismal state; it shows how important the pope considered the proper performance of the sacrament of baptism. The same letter raised a related issue about whether one might make liturgical offerings for the dead. Gregory affirmed the practice on behalf of genuine believers, but reiterated that one might not do so for unbelievers, including dead pagan ancestors, nor was it legitimate to raise pagans from their graves and baptize them in death.[29]

The extent of the difficulties and dangers that Boniface faced in the mission-field and the complexities of the cultural contexts in which he tried to work came sharply into focus at the end of his life. Travelling back to the northern shores of Frisia, where he had first preached the gospel to unbelievers, Boniface encountered a group of seaborne raiders who martyred him and his companions on the shore at Dokkum in June 754. His devotion to mission and catechesis earned him a martyr's crown.

Conclusion

What lessons can we take from these reflections on the ways that Boniface and other early missionaries among Germanic peoples approached the hitherto stony and barren hearts of their contemporaries? Two overarching themes come to mind. Firstly, the issue of language and the necessity of translating the words and teachings of scripture and liturgy into the vernacular.

All these clerics recognized that language could provide a barrier to the acceptance of belief, and so sought means of communication in terms that would resonate among the people. That translation needed to be made not only in linguistic but also cultural terms; the new faith was as alien to the social practices of the pagans (especially but not exclusively their treatment of the dead) as it was to their native tongue. In our own context we need to be sensitive to how the languages of the Church may not always resonate in contemporary culture. Secondly, we should not overlook the repeated focus in these narratives on the central importance of baptism, of bringing people to the font and ensuring that the crucial sacrament was performed correctly. The arguments that evangelists employed to bring unbelievers to the waters of salvation were cast consistently in direct antithesis to their pagan beliefs, specifically to their faith in a pantheon of gods. The Saxon baptismal promise proved particularly revealing here, in its insistence that neophytes give up the gods whom they once had worshipped. It might be profitable for us to think about the nature of the obstacles that might prevent new believers from turning to faith today. We might ponder which are the 'old gods' of our society that we ask believers to reject and lay aside before they can come and meet the living God, who creates, redeems and sanctifies all things.

Notes

1 Daniel, Letter to Boniface 723/4, in M. Tangl, ed., *Die Briefe des heiligen Bonifatius*, no. 23; E. Emerton, trans., *The Letters of Boniface*, no. 15 (New York: Colmbia University Press, 1940).

2 Emerton, *The Letters of Boniface*, no. 15.

3 Malcolm Lambert, *Christians and Pagans* (New Haven, CT: Yale University Press, 2010), provides an excellent survey of Christianity in Roman and post-Roman Britain.

4 Bede, *Ecclesiastical History* I. 23–4.

5 Bede, *Ecclesiastical History* I. 25.

6 Gregory the Great, *Letter* 8.28 (July 598), P. Ewald and L. M. Hartmann, eds, MGH Epistolae 1–2, 2 vols (Berlin: Weidmann,

1887–99), Vol. 2, pp. 30–1; John R. C. Martyn, trans., *The Letters of Gregory the Great*, 3 vols (Toronto: Pontifical Institute of Medieval Studies), Vol. 2, pp. 523–4.

7 Bede, *Ecclesiastical History* I. 32.

8 Bede, *Ecclesiastical History* I. 30.

9 Bede, *Ecclesiastical History* II. 9.

10 Bede, *Ecclesiastical History* II. 10.

11 Bede, *Ecclesiastical History* II. 11.

12 Bede, *Ecclesiastical History* II. 12.

13 Bede, *Ecclesiastical History* II. 13.

14 Bede, *Ecclesiastical History* IV. 13.

15 Bede, *Ecclesiastical History* II. 5.

16 Bede, *Ecclesiastical History* II. 6.

17 Bede, *Ecclesiastical History* III. 1.

18 Bede, *Ecclesiastical History* II. 20.

19 Stephen, *Life of Wilfrid*, ch. 26; Bertram Colgrave, ed. and trans., *The Life of Bishop Wilfrid by Eddius Stephanus* (Cambridge: Cambridge University Press, 1927), pp. 52–3.

20 Miriam Adan Jones, 'The language of baptism in early Anglo-Saxon England: the case for Old English', *Studies in Church History* 53 (2017), pp. 39–50.

21 Rob Meens, 'With one foot in the font: the failed baptism of the Frisian king Radbod and the 8th-century discussion about the fate of unbaptized forefathers', in Pádraic Moran and Immo Warntjes (eds), *Early Medieval Ireland and Europe: Chronology, Contacts, Scholarship: Festschrift for Dáibhí Ó Cróinín* (Turnhout: Brepols, 2015), pp. 577–96.

22 Theodore, *Penitential*, I. xv; Text U, P. W. Finsterwalder, ed., *Die Canones Theodori Cantuariensis und ihre Überlieferungsformen* (Weimar: H. Böhlaus, 1929), pp. 310–11; J. T. McNeill and H. M. Gamer, trans., *Medieval Handbooks of Penance* (New York: Columbia University Press, 1938), p. 198.

23 *Penitential*, II.xii.18-19, Text U, ed. Finsterwalder, p. 328; trans. McNeill and Gamer, p. 210.

24 *Penitential*, II.i.4-5, Text U, ed. Finsterwalder, p. 312; trans. McNeill and Gamer, p. 199.

25 Bede, *Ecclesiastical History* IV. 13.

26 *Life of Wulfram*, Ch. 9, W. Levison, ed., MGH SS rer. Merov. 5 (Hanover and Leipzig: Hahn, 1910), pp. 661–73, at p. 668; Meens, 'With one foot in the font', p. 579.

27 Meens, 'With one foot in the font'.

28 Bede, *Ecclesiastical History* V. 10.

29 Pope Gregory III, Letter to Boniface (732); Tangl, ed., *Die Briefe*, no. 28; transl. Emerton, *Letters of Boniface*, no. 20.

8

Rooted in the Bible and history: How the creeds can help with faith formation

ALISTER MCGRATH

The Apostles' Creed opens with the Latin word *credo*, which is almost always translated as 'I believe'. Yet the proper meaning of *credo* at the time when the creeds were written was 'to trust or confide in a person or thing; to have confidence in; to trust.'[1] While we now tend to think of faith in terms of a theoretical judgement, the creeds see it as a personal commitment. Faustus of Riez, writing in the fifth century, explains that to believe (*credere*) in God means to 'respond to God in worship and adoration, by giving ourselves and our affections completely over to God'.[2] Part of that devotion is what I like to call the 'discipleship of the mind',[3] which aims to help us develop habits of thought that are rooted in the realities of the Christian faith, rather than passively echoing the dominant ideas of our culture.

'Catechesis' may be a slightly unwieldy and cumbersome word, yet it designates a process of immersion in the Christian faith that enables us to love God with our minds, and not merely with our hearts. Christian discipleship is about deepening our commitment to and understanding of the gospel. The New Testament views faith (*pistis*) primarily as relational trust, but nevertheless understands this to include specific grounding and informing beliefs.[4] Catechesis is a process of disciplined immersion in the Christian faith, in which we gradually come to grasp its intellectual, moral, and spiritual riches. While the education of believers is important at every level, it is particularly important in the case of those who are transitioning to Christianity from a settled attitude of unbelief or commitment to another religious tradition. How does their faith in Christ relate to their previous ways of thinking and acting?

The New Testament uses the term *metanoia* – traditionally but inadequately translated as 'repentance' – to refer to a process of mental realignment and recalibration, in which our natural or inherited ways of thinking about ourselves and our world are transformed by an interplay of divine grace and human reflection. We can thus think of Christianity both encouraging and enabling a discipleship of the mind, supplementing a discipleship of the heart and of the hands. Catechesis is thus an instrument of spiritual growth, providing a framework that can be developed and enriched spiritually and relationally.

We need to make sure that we never think of Christianity as simply assent to a set of ideas. There is something deeper. Christian doctrines – or, more accurately, the larger Christian picture of which they are individual parts – help us to avoid the failure that the poet T. S. Eliot warned about – namely, having an experience but missing its proper meaning. We need a framework of interpretation that helps us to understand what a story or experience really means. Otherwise, to draw on the well-known line from Shakespeare's *Macbeth*, life simply becomes a tale that is 'full of sound and fury, signifying nothing'.

Believing: expanding our vision of faith

In uttering the credal words 'I believe', Christians declare that they have discovered a place of refuge, a safe anchorage for the soul, a way of seeing the world that makes sense, and a firm place on which they may stand. The first declaration of the creeds is thus not so much an item of belief, but an assertion of the need for faith to lead a meaningful life in the first place. For the Christian, faith is both trusting that there is a 'big picture' of life, and a decision and commitment to step inside this way of seeing ourselves and our world, and live it out. It enfolds a way of understanding our world, and a commitment to live and think on its basis, as we find ourselves transformed in and through our faith.

Yet it is not simply Christians who 'believe', as if every other religious, ethical, political or social conviction is rigorously grounded in the evidence. Any moral, political, religious, or anti-religious worldview demands faith, in that its core beliefs cannot be demonstrated to be true. As the Greek philosopher Xenophanes argued, life involves a 'woven web of guesses'. To hold to any belief or moral value is to *judge* that these are true and trustworthy, while knowing that they cannot be proved. I recall my growing sense of dismay when I realized that my youthful atheism, which I had fondly believed to be self-evidently true, was actually a judgement – an interpretation of the world, rather than an evidentially compelling factual statement about it. As Karl Popper pointed out, the natural sciences often find themselves in a similar position: all scientific 'theories are, and remain hypotheses: they are conjecture (*doxa*) as opposed to indubitable knowledge (*episteme*)'.[5]

My own experience of catechesis was neither spiritually inspiring nor spiritually illuminating. I grew up in Ireland, and have strong memories of being taught the old Prayer Book Catechism at the Parish Church of St Margaret's, Downpatrick, around the year 1960. I can still remember extracts from that Catechism which were instilled within me. While this can be seen as a tribute to the capacity of learning by rote to impress phrases in my mind, it was probably a cause of my subsequent aggressive atheist phase as a teenager. I was being fed phrases and ideas that seemed meaningless, lacking any traction on the real questions that I had about the meaning of life and my place in a strange and vast universe. If I learned anything about faith, it was only in the sense of an imposed absorption of words, without any sense of their meaning or importance.

My rediscovery of Christianity while a student at Oxford University forced me to re-open questions I had assumed were closed and settled. In my own case, what drew me back to Christianity was a 'perfect storm' of my growing realization of the intellectual fragility of atheism, and an increasing suspicion that Christianity possessed an intellectual depth and resilience that I had failed to grasp – and hence had somewhat prematurely assumed did not exist.

Although I was aware of the existential bleakness of atheism as a teenager, I had persuaded myself that truth was often austere and challenging. I simply needed to accept that our world was either meaningless or that I could defiantly impose a meaning of my own invention upon it. Yet doubts were creeping in about the resilience of my atheism, which I was increasingly coming to see as a *belief* that there was no God, rather than – as I had once thought – an evidentially secure and rationally incontestable conclusion that any reasonable person would be compelled to accept.

Oxford was perhaps an ideal place at which to discover the intellectual richness of Christianity in the early 1970s, not least because of the presence of a substantial number of Christian students who had thought carefully about their faith, and were prepared to explain and justify it to people like myself. I have no doubt that other Christian students had a genuine and fulfilling faith; it was just that they seemed a little vague about its intellectual content, and unwilling to talk to someone who wanted to explore some genuine – if difficult – questions. Looking back, it seems to me that some had taken the trouble to think through their faith, considering both its basis and its outcomes. Perhaps others had taught them about their faith; or perhaps they had taught themselves, by reading the Christian self-help manuals of the time – such as C. S. Lewis's *Mere Christianity*, or John Stott's *Basic Christianity*. These students knew what they believed, and why they believed it. They were confident about their faith, and were capable of presenting it intelligently and clearly.

Catechesis matters if Christians are to grow in their faith, and to be able to explain its substance and outcomes to those who lie beyond the community of faith. Yet it is also about the expansion of our vision of faith – a process of deepening and widening our initial grasp of faith. There is a 'big picture' to be discovered, which goes far beyond the limited and impoverished view of things that results from skimming the surface of reality. The creed of many around us may be 'What you see is what you get.' Yet the Christian creeds invite us – to use some words of C. S. Lewis – to go 'further up and further in', discovering and experiencing a deeper and richer understanding of reality.

Yet recognizing the importance of catechesis does not answer what is perhaps one of the most important questions that needs to be engaged: how is catechesis best to be done? In this chapter, I shall focus on the specific question of how the creeds can help the churches develop catechetical ministries, as well as encourage individuals to go deeper in their faith. Yet since this approach can too easily collapse into demands for learning creeds by rote, we need to re-imagine their purpose and role. In what follows, I shall develop this point further.

Re-imagining the creeds

Visual images are important in allowing us to explore complex themes, often offering imaginative or intuitive ways of discerning interconnections that are much more difficult to identity and explore using purely logical or conceptual approaches. In my own teaching and preaching ministry, I have increasingly found it helpful and productive to present the creeds as maps of the landscape of faith.[6] This is hardly a new idea; it has been used regularly in the past by writers such as C. S. Lewis, and has been developed as a tool for historical research in some important areas of theology – such as the interdisciplinary field of science and religion.[7]

In developing this analogy, I invite my audiences to imagine that they find themselves on an island. Perhaps they have been shipwrecked there (*Robinson Crusoe* or *The Coral Island* come to mind); or perhaps they have landed on the island as part of a tour of the eastern Mediterranean, or the Caribbean. Naturally, they want to explore this new place – and so need a guide. This might take the form of a map, showing the main features of the island, and where they are located. The map itself cannot disclose the beauty, wonder, or history of those places; yet it is not meant to. It is an invitation to *discover* them, and then to *explore* them.

This image helps us re-imagine the process of catechesis, allowing us to gain a better understanding of two of its major functions in the life of the Church – namely, introducing newcomers to the Christian faith to its core themes, and helping those who are already Christians deepen their understanding of their faith. Let's sketch the scenario that helps us imagine each of these in a new way.

The novelist Evelyn Waugh is probably best known for his bestseller *Brideshead Revisited* (1945). In 1930, Waugh made the decision to convert to Catholicism. He later wrote to a friend describing how his new faith allowed him to see things clearly for the first time. It was as if he had left behind a distorted and illusory realm of shadows, and embraced and entered a strange and wonderful new world. And having stepped into that world, Waugh began 'the delicious process of exploring it limitlessly'.[8]

That's the process I experienced as I began to explore the Christian faith following my conversion back in 1971. I was coming across ideas – such as the doctrine of the Trinity – which I had never thought about before, and trying to make sense of them. It often occurred to me that I was like Robinson Crusoe – someone who had landed on a strange island, and was trying to work out what its resources were, and how I might survive there.

One way, of course, was to read books written by those who already knew the island well, and in effect could offer me travellers guides to its features, helping me adapt to this new landscape and settle down. C. S. Lewis's *Mere Christianity* is a good example of this work, and many other examples could be added.[9] Yet there is another way – talking to those who already live on the island, and learning from them. The process of catechesis is about the transition from being a newcomer to being an inhabitant of this landscape of faith. It involves immersion in a community, in which newcomers absorb the community's ethos, values, and goals, gradually forming their own distinct individual understanding and enactment of the Christian faith.

C. S. Lewis, reflecting on his own experience of spiritual growth and theological reflection, remarked that 'the one really adequate instrument for learning about God is the Christian community'.[10] It is within such a community of people 'united together in a body, loving one another, helping one another, showing [God] to one another' that the life of faith takes root and develops. Although Lewis found his faith stimulated and enriched in other ways – most notably, through the group of colleagues that we know as 'the Inklings' – there is no doubting the importance he attached to the Church as a means of grace.

Yet while catechesis plays an important role in helping those who are new to the Christian landscape to find their bearings, it also meets a significant need in encouraging long-term inhabitants of this landscape of faith to know it better – for example, by enabling people who are familiar with the individual elements of the Christian faith to get a sense of the 'big picture' that lies behind them. Christians need to grasp how each individual belief or doctrine offers its own distinct 'little picture' that turns out to be an integral part of the 'big picture'.

Imagine you are standing on an alpine peak, and looking down at a breathtaking sunlit landscape. After a few moments, during which you are held captive by its beauty and scale, you decide to try and capture the scene. You start taking photographs – a few panoramic shots, followed by more detailed studies of the woods, mountains, streams, and towns you can see. Yet each of these snapshots fits into the panorama, which allow you to see how each belongs in its own place within the bigger picture. The big picture positions and contextualizes the snapshots, confirming the coherence and unity of the landscape as a whole.

To make sense of individual snapshots of an alpine vista, we need to first take in the greater panorama, which positions and contextualizes each of these smaller pictures, allowing us to see them as part of a greater coherent whole. Similarly, to understand individual Christian beliefs, we must first catch sight of the greater vision, of which they are part. Now there is nothing wrong with snapshots, which often provide welcome detail of complex landscapes. Yet there is clearly a danger that certain approaches to catechesis just offer us those snapshots, and fail to show us the panorama.

Christian beliefs are not like a set of individual, unrelated ideas. We cannot think of Christianity as a series of isolated boxes containing individual ideas – such as creation, incarnation, salvation, and the Trinity. These ideas are interconnected, like a web, held together by the compelling and persuasive vision of reality that is made possible by the Christian gospel. The image of a web points to a series of interconnected strands of belief, which is stronger and more robust than any of its individual parts. To study any single doctrinal theme is actually to study the whole web of faith as it intersects at this node, or as it focuses on this specific theme. Christian doctrines are connected together, supporting and informing each other. They lead onto and into each other, so that the explorer can set out from any landmark in the landscape of faith, and find that the paths taken will lead to all the others.

Discovering the coherence of the Christian faith

Let's come back to the image of a map of an island landscape. Such a map will show towns that are connected by roads. The map helps us to realize that we can visit every town on the island through this network of roads, radiating outward from each of these hubs towards its neighbours. We cannot study individual Christian beliefs in isolation, but need to appreciate the coherence of Christian doctrine. Each element is woven into the fabric of faith. As Christians reflect on the significance of Jesus Christ, they find themselves linking up with related ideas, such as the doctrine of God, the idea of salvation, and understanding of human nature.

The individual threads of Christian belief can thus be woven together to disclose a pattern – a pattern that could not be seen by considering any single thread in isolation. We cannot speak of the Christian understanding of the identity of Jesus Christ without reflecting on the nature of God, the nature of salvation, the role of the Holy Spirit, or our understanding of human nature – to mention just the more obvious themes, to which others can easily be added.

The creeds thus identify the constituent threads of Christian belief, and invite us to weave them together into a coherent 'big picture'. It is this vision as a whole – rather than any of its individual details – which proves so persuasive and compelling, appealing to the imagination, not merely the reason. The big picture comes first; the details come later. The Christian faith allows us to see patterns in the apparent chaos of our world; to perceive a melody, when others only hear a noise. Instead of being overwhelmed with *information*, we are enabled to discern *meaning*. Catechesis must never be allowed to focus exclusively on individual beliefs; we need to grasp its 'big picture'. As psychologists have emphasized for some time, what really matters to people is a sense that the world is coherent, and that they can make a difference to its direction and development.[11]

The creeds are primarily communal Christian confessions of faith, setting out the vision of reality that has given – and still gives – life, purpose and direction to individual believers and to the Christian community down the ages. When I recite the creeds, I think of myself as doing three things. First, I am calling to mind the 'big picture' that underlies the Christian faith, which helps me make sense of my world and life. Second, I am affirming that I am part of a believing community, which sees this document as mapping out the beliefs that make it distinctive. I thus see myself as an inhabitant of the landscape of faith, not a tourist or an outside observer. And third, I am recognizing that, in embracing Christianity, I am declaring my willingness to discover and explore what I have not yet encountered, refusing to be limited by my present understanding of my faith.

The creeds are thus aspirational and invitational, giving us a framework for both exploring its individual themes and discovering the greater reality of which they are part. To borrow an image from Teresa of Ávila, the Christian faith is like a mansion, with many rooms to explore. Most of us, however, fail to progress beyond the entrance hall. The creeds map out this mansion of faith, encouraging us to become familiar with its many rooms, and learn to live in them.

One of the most important functions of the creeds is to challenge individualist versions of the Christian faith. 'This is the way I see it – so this is the way things are.' All of us have our own personal creeds, adapted to our needs yet limited by our perspectives and concerns. Yet the creeds transcend these limits placed on the capacity of any one individual fully to take in the vast landscape of the Christian faith. C. S. Lewis realized that his own grasp of faith was enriched by entering into the visual frame of other people. His limited personal vision was thus extended, expanded, and enriched. 'My own eyes are not enough for me, I will see through those of others. . . . Like the night sky in the Greek poem, I see with a myriad eyes, but it is still I who see.'[12] That's why reading Christian classics is such an important component of the ongoing process of catechesis.

The creeds are thus communal documents that bear witness to what Christians down the ages have found to be trustworthy and authentic readings of the Christian faith. They are there to help us by questioning our own personal grasp of our faith, and to enrich us by showing us what more there is to discover and appreciate. They do not suppress our individuality, but enable us to grasp something that our individual limits prevent us from seeing fully. They thus help a Church that has become preoccupied with 'relevance' to relearn a forgotten way of doing things and recapture lost attitudes, arousing the echoes of a rich past to enrich the present.

Four questions about Christian beliefs

Christian reflection on the place of doctrines in the life of faith ought to involve focusing on four questions. First, what do Christians believe? Second, what are the reasons for believing that a certain doctrine is true? Third, how can they best be expressed and communicated? And fourth, if these doctrines are true and trustworthy, what are their implications? What difference does the Christian faith make to the way in which we understand our world, and act within it? What new or distinctive way of seeing things does it enable, and how does this affect the way in which we live in the world? Is it rich enough and stable enough to be able to offer something distinctive to the world without being captured by the world?

Catechesis often focuses only on the first of these, inviting us to absorb what Christians believe. Yet the recent rise of the New Atheism of Richard Dawkins and others makes it painfully clear that is not enough to be able to explain what Christians believe: those ideas need to be explained and justified to a sceptical (but not necessarily hostile) culture. And, as every preacher knows, Christian ideas need to be communicated, using engaging and informing images and narratives. Yet my main concern relates to the fourth aspect of Christian belief: we need to encourage people to look *through*, not simply look *at*, Christian beliefs.

One of the best accounts of this point is found in the writings of the poet-theologian George Herbert. In his poem 'The Elixir', Herbert uses the analogy of looking through a glass window to illustrate the transformative potential of the gospel. We can look at a window; but we are really meant to look through it.[13]

A man that looks on glass,
On it may stay his eye;
Or if he pleaseth, through it pass,
And then the heav'n espy.

Herbert here contrasts two quite different possible modes of engagement with a piece of glass – a 'looking on' and a 'passing through'. I might look at a window, seeing it as an object of interest in itself, perhaps focusing on the quality of its glass. Yet there is a deeper way of interacting with this window. We can *look through it,* rather than *look at it,* thus using this window as a means of gaining access to what lies beyond it. The window now functions as a *gateway to vision,* rather than being itself the *object of vision.* It becomes a means of gaining access to a greater reality, rather than being the object of study itself.

Herbert's point is that the Christian faith makes possible a new way of seeing things, throwing open the shutters on a world that cannot be fully or properly known, experienced or encountered through human wisdom and strength alone. Christian doctrine offers us a subject worthy of study in its own right; yet its supreme importance lies in its capacity to allow us to pass through its imaginative gateway, and behold our world in a new way. For Herbert, Christian doctrine aims to make us into faithful disciples, in that it helps us to understand our faith and grow in wisdom by developing habits of thought and action that faithfully reflect and communicate the Christian gospel. Catechesis serves its purpose best in enabling this process of seeing life and the world through a Christian lens – not simply looking at that lens as an end in itself.

Yet Herbert's image of glass can be developed in another way. A lens is a piece of glass that enhances the capacity of human vision – as in a telescope or microscope. Galileo famously discovered that a telescope enabled him to look at the night sky, and behold sights that none had seen before him – such as the craters and seas of the moon, and the myriad of stars within the Milky Way. The Christian faith, as set out in the creeds, is like a telescope that enhances the reach of our natural vision so that we can glimpse something of God. As Austin Farrer once put it, we 'see through the Church of Christ' as someone 'sees through the telescope to the stars'.[14]

The image of a telescope is helpful in another way. I might be walking along a sandy beach on a beautiful day, surveying the deep blue ocean, stretching far into the distance. I might notice something moving on the horizon, and use a telescope to see what it is. To begin with, I see only a shapeless and fuzzy blur. Yet as I bring the image into focus, the shapeless blur is transformed into a crisp and vibrant image of a yacht in full sail. We can think of the Christian faith as a lens that brings the meaning of life into focus. Secularism offers a rather different lens, which lets us see less – and thus persuades some that there is less to be seen.

Some might see human life as 'a tale told by an idiot, full of sound and fury, signifying nothing'. We might think of the young Joy Davidman, who summarized her early loss of faith in a neat aphorism: 'In 1929 I believed in nothing but American prosperity; in 1930 I believed in nothing.'[15] Yet using the wrong lens means that the world *seems* out of focus and distorted. We need a new lens if we are to see things more clearly. What some see as something random, meaningless and chaotic, without any underlying order or significance, is brought into focus and given meaning and value by the imaginative theological framework of the Christian faith.

As the philosopher Ludwig Wittgenstein pointed out, faith in God brings life into focus, and conveys meaning through helping us realize that we are thinking and living in accordance with something deeper and greater than ourselves. 'In order to live happily I must be in agreement with the world. And that is what "being happy" means.'[16] We need to grasp the 'big picture' of the universe, and position ourselves within it, accepting any challenges it may bring to the glib and shallow notions of human goodness and autonomy that have become embedded as unexamined cultural norms.

Yet some people prefer to keep seeing the world through a distorting lens. The philosopher Iris Murdoch pointed out that we often shield ourselves from reality by 'fabricating an anxious, usually self-preoccupied, often falsifying *veil* which partially conceals the world'.[17] The true meaning of things is sometimes too disturbing for our comfort. As T. S. Eliot famously remarked, 'humankind cannot bear very much reality'.

Catechesis and mystery

The human mind struggles to take in the vastness of our universe. The great physicist Werner Heisenberg argued that scientific thinking 'always hovers over a bottomless depth', given the limits placed on human understanding.[18] We are confronted with the 'impenetrable darkness' of the universe, and our difficulties as we struggle to find a language adequate to engage and represent this.[19] Our universe is a mystery – something with so many impenetrable and uncomprehended dimensions that our minds simply cannot take it in.

It is important for anyone doing catechesis to emphasize that we have to learn to live with mystery. Our minds struggle to even begin to cope with the immensity and majesty of God. The sheer vastness of God – traditionally expressed using the notion of 'glory' – causes images and words falter, if not break down completely, as we try to depict God fully and faithfully. That's why the notion of 'mystery' is so important. A mystery is not something that is irrational, but is something that exceeds reason's capacity to discern and describe – thus transcending, rather than contradicting, reason. We can only cope with such a mystery either by filtering out what little we can grasp, and hope that the rest is unimportant; or by reducing it to what our minds can accommodate and thus reduce it to the rationally manageable. Yet both these strategies distort, disfigure and mislead.

For many outside the Christian community – and, dare I say it, also for some within it – the doctrine of the Trinity is a classic instance of the irrationality of faith. Yet Augustine of Hippo pointed out that, if we can get our minds around something, it can't be God. Anything that we can grasp fully and completely *cannot* be God, precisely because it would be so limited and impoverished if it can be fully grasped by the human mind. As Augustine remarked, '*Si comprehendis non est Deus.*' If you can get your mind around it, it's not God.

A probably apocryphal story about Augustine in the early fifth century makes this point rather nicely. Augustine was bishop of Hippo Regius, a Roman coastal town in North Africa. While writing his major work *On the Trinity*, he decided to take a break and went for a stroll along the beautiful beaches nearby. As he walked, he came across a young boy behaving rather strangely. Over and over again, the boy went to the edge of the shoreline, filled a spoon with seawater, and then emptied this into a hole in the sand.

Augustine watched this diverting scene for some time, mystified. What was the boy doing? Eventually, he decided to ask. The boy pointed to the Mediterranean Sea and informed Augustine of his intention to empty the entire ocean into his hole in the sand. Augustine dismissed this. 'You can't do that! You'll never fit the ocean into that tiny space.' The boy is supposed to have replied: 'And you're wasting your time writing a book about God. You'll never fit God into a book!'

Now some questions probably need to be asked about the historical reliability of this story! But whether it is true or not, it makes a point that we simply cannot evade as we try to wrestle with God. In the end, our minds just aren't big enough to cope with the conceptual vastness of God, so brilliantly expressed in the theological notion of 'glory'. God simply overwhelms our mental capacities through what John Donne termed 'the exceeding weight of glory'.[20]

This is an important point to make in catechesis. Christian doctrines try to capture and safeguard something far greater. The creeds are hedges, enfolding and protecting the rich pastureland of faith; they are fences, safeguarding the wells of living water that sustain the life of faith. They are closed caskets of treasure, which we are invited to open and explore. The catechist has to convey the difference between the vessel and what it contains; between the words and the greater realities of faith.

Over the years, I have developed great respect for the Czech philosopher and theologian Tomáš Halík, who constantly highlighted that we come to terms with the depth and the mystery of reality, including the question of God. When writing his books, Halík often withdrew to a hermitage deep in a Rhineland forest, and came to see the forest itself as an 'apt metaphor for religious mystery'. The forest is deep and broad, an 'unfinished symphony of nature', consisting of multiple layers of reality, which cannot be reduced to a collection of individual trees.[21] The individual trees matter, and deserve to be appreciated for what they are; yet we cannot overlook the still greater reality of the forest, which transcends those individual trees.

We can grasp God and the things of God in part, and reliably so – but not *totally* so. As the great Puritan writer Richard Baxter once remarked, we may well *know* God; yet to *comprehend* God lies beyond our capacity.[22] Yet the catechist can point out the upside of the glory, majesty, and vastness of God. Yes, these make it difficult for us to take God in fully. But they also lead us to worship – the natural response of a believer to an appreciation of the glory of God. The catechist has the task of inviting us to appreciate both trees and the forest, becoming acquainted with the individual elements of our faith, while at the same time pointing to the greater reality, the bigger picture, which lies beyond them.

Conclusion

This chapter has explored the role of the creeds in the process of faith formation that is traditionally known as 'catechesis'. It remains a major ministry of the Church, both in terms of helping those who are new to faith to find their way, and those who are Christian 'dwellers' to expand their vision of their faith. The creeds map out the landscape of faith that needs to be explored, in order that we may settle down within it. While some may commend learning these creeds by heart, the approach set out in this chapter invites us to re-imagine their function, and see them as maps to help us find our way within this landscape, and ensure we discover and appreciate its riches. Yet perhaps most importantly of all, this chapter has stressed the role of the Church and individual Christians in helping others to grasp the Christian gospel in all its fullness, and not simply its individual elements.

Notes

1 C. T. Lewis and C. Short, *A Latin Dictionary* (Oxford: Oxford University Press, 1891), p. 479.

2 Faustus of Riez, *On the Holy Spirit*, I, 1.

3 Alister McGrath, *Mere Discipleship: On Growing in Faith and Wisdom* (London: SPCK, 2018).

4 Teresa Morgan, *Roman Faith and Christian Faith: Pistis and Fides in the Early Roman Empire and Early Churches* (Oxford: Oxford University Press, 2015), p. 508. Morgan points out how the Christian notion of 'faith' is too easily assimilated to cultural analogues – such as 'belief', 'persuasion', or 'conviction' – thus losing its distinct focus.

5 Karl Popper, *Conjectures and Refutations*, 2nd edn (London: Routledge & Kegan Paul, 1965), pp. 103–4.

6 For a detailed account, see Alister McGrath, *The Landscape of Faith: An Explorer's Guide to the Christian Creeds* (London: SPCK, 2018).

7 See, for example, Peter Harrison, *The Territories of Science and Religion* (Chicago: University of Chicago Press, 2015).

8 Letter to Edward Sackville-West, cited in Michael de-la-Noy, *Eddy: The Life of Edward Sackville-West* (London: Bodley Head, 1988), p. 237.

9 Such as John Stott, *Basic Christianity* (Downers Grove, IL: Intervarsity Press, 2013); Rowan Williams, *Tokens of Trust: An Introduction to Christian Belief* (Norwich: Canterbury, 2007); or Tom Wright, *Simply Christian* (London: SPCK, 2011).

10 C. S. Lewis, *Mere Christianity* (London: HarperCollins, 2002), p. 165.

11 There is a very large literature on this theme. A good entry point is Joshua A. Hicks and Laura A. King, 'Meaning in Life and Seeing the Big Picture: Positive Affect and Global Focus', in *Cognition and Emotion* 21, no. 7 (2007), pp. 1577–84.

12 C. S. Lewis, *An Experiment in Criticism* (Cambridge: Cambridge University Press, 1992), pp. 137, 140–1.

13 George Herbert, *Works*, F. E. Hutchinson, ed. (Oxford: Clarendon Press, 1941), p. 184.

14 Austin Farrer, 'On Being an Anglican', in *The End of Man* (London: SPCK, 1973), pp. 48–52; quote at p. 52.

15 Joy Davidman, *Out of My Bone: The Letters of Joy Davidman* (Grand Rapids, MI: Eerdmans, 2009), p. 86.

16 Ludwig Wittgenstein, *Notebooks, 1914–1916* (New York: Harper, 1961), p. 75.

17 Iris Murdoch, *The Sovereignty of Good* (London: Routledge, 2001), p. 82.

18 Werner Heisenberg, *Die Ordnung der Wirklichkeit* (Munich: Piper Verlag, 1989), p. 44.

19 Heisenberg, *Die Ordnung der Wirklichkeit*, p. 44.

20 John Donne, *Selections from Divine Poems, Sermons, Devotions, and Prayers*, John Booty, ed. (Mahwah, NJ: Paulist Press International, 1990), p. 172.

21 Tomáš Halík, *Night of the Confessor: Christian Faith in an Age of Uncertainty* (New York: Image Books, 2012), p. 19.

22 *The Practical Works of Richard Baxter*, 23 vols (London: James Duncan, 1830), Vol. 13, p. 29.

Conclusion:
The renewal of catechesis today

STEVEN CROFT

And finally . . .

At the beginning of Acts 19, Luke paints one of the most dramatic pictures in the New Testament. The apostle Paul arrives alone in Ephesus, the great metropolis at the crossroads between East and West, the centre of the cult of the goddess Artemis and the gateway to the Roman provinces in Asia Minor.

The mission to Ephesus will last for three years: it will be the last and the most fruitful of Paul's missionary encounters. It is built on catechesis.

As a result of Paul's ministry, all the residents of Asia heard the word of the Lord (19.10). There is a public burning of occult books (19.19). The whole economy of the region is transformed and the livelihood of the silversmiths threatened in such a way that they lead a city wide riot (19.23).

The lesson of this ministry is that deep social and economic transformation begins with deep Christian formation and the renewal of catechesis.

Paul begins with the incomplete formation of the embryonic Christian community who have been offered a partial version of the Christian faith. The twelve disciples confess: 'We have not even heard that there is a Holy Spirit' (19.2). They are baptized into the name of Jesus, Paul prays for them and they are filled with the Spirit. There is a new Pentecost.

Paul teaches next in the synagogue, following his normal pattern. When he is ejected 'he left them, taking the disciples with him, and argued daily in the lecture hall of Tyrannus. This continued for two years so that all the residents of Asia, both Jews and Greeks, heard the word of the Lord' (19.9–10).

As Paul refers back to his three-year ministry in Ephesus he refers three times to its foundation in his ministry of teaching – of catechesis (Acts 20.20, 27, 31).

As we look to the future of our own nation and the renewal of the mission and ministry of God's Church, there is no greater priority than the thoughtful, deep, prayerful and compassionate renewal of the ministry of catechesis for our own day.

Our calling is to see Christ formed in the lives of new believers, to see children, women and men rooted and grounded in love. May God bless this renewal of catechesis in our own day as in previous generations for the sake of the Church and also for the sake of God's world.

References and further reading

A very short history of catechesis

Atwell, Robert, Stephen Cottrell, Steven Croft and Paula Gooder, *The Pilgrim Course* (2014) and *Pilgrim: the Way of Faith* (2017), London: Church House Publishing. See also www.pilgrimcourse.org.

Duffy, Eamon, *The Stripping of the Altars* (New Haven, CT: Yale University Press, 1992).

Green, Ian, *The Christian's ABC, Catechisms and Catechizing in England, 1530–1740* (New York: Clarendon Press, 1996).

Harmless, William, *Augustine and the Catechumenate* (Collegeville, MI: Pueblo, 1995).

Harrison, Carol, *The Art of Listening in the Early Church* (Oxford: Oxford University Press, 2013).

Perham, Michael, *On the Way* (London: Church House Publishing, 1995).

Worship transforming catechesis: Catechesis transforming worship

Common Worship: Christian Initiation (London: Church House Publishing, 2006).

Johnson, Maxwell, *The Rites of Christian Initiation* (Collegeville, MI: Pueblo, 2007).

Jones, Simon, *Celebrating Christian Initiation* (London: SPCK, 2016).

Kreider, Alan, *The Change of Conversion and the Origin of Christendom* (Eugene, OR: Wipf & Stock, 1999).

Millar, Sandra, *Life Events* (London: Church House Publishing, 2018).

Spinks, Bryan, *Early and Medieval Rituals and Theologies of Baptism* (London: Ashgate, 2006).

Yarnold, Edward, *The Awe-Inspiring Rites of Initiation* (Edinburgh: T&T Clark, 1994).

Charismatic catechesis

Augustine

Confessions, Maria Boulding (transl.), *Works of Saint Augustine* 1.1 (Hyde Park, NY: New City Press, 1997).

On Christian Doctrine, D. W. Robertson (transl.), Library of Liberal Arts 80 (Indianapolis: Bobbs-Merrill, 1958).

On Teaching Beginners in the Faith, Raymond Canning (transl.), *Works of Saint Augustine* 1.10 (Hyde Park, NY: New City Press, 2006).

Gregory of Nyssa

'Gregory of Nyssa, Against Eunomius, Book 3' in Johan Leemans and Matthieu Cassin (eds), Stuart G. Hall (transl.), Gregory of Nyssa: *Contra Eunomium III* An English Translation with Commentary and Supporting Studies. Proceedings of the 12th International Colloquium on Gregory of Nyssa. Supplements of Vigiliae Christianae 124 (Leiden, Boston: Brill, 2010).

Julian of Norwich

Showings, Edmund Colledge and James Walsh (transl.), *The Classics of Western Spirituality* (London: SPCK, 1978).

Harrison, Carol, *The Art of Listening in the Early Church* (Oxford: Oxford University Press, 2013).

Making Christians and lifelong catechesis

Dunn, James D. G. (ed.), *The Cambridge Companion to St Paul* (Cambridge: Cambridge University Press, 2003).

Ferguson, Everett, *The Early Church at Work and Worship: Catechesis, Baptism, Eschatology, and Martyrdom* (Cambridge: James Clarke & Co., 2014).

Johnson, Maxwell E., *Praying and Believing in Early Christianity* (Collegeville, MN: Liturgical Press, 2013).

Kreider, Alan, *The Patient Ferment of the Early Church* (Grand Rapids, MI: Baker Academic, 2016).

Strawbridge, Jennifer R., *The Pauline Effect: The Use of the Pauline Epistles by Early Christian Writers* (Berlin: De Gruyter, 2015).

Praying the Psalms of David with Christ

Adams, Cocksworth, Collicutt *et al.*, *Reflections on the Psalms* (London: Church House Publishing, 2015). Devotional reflections on every psalm taken from contributors to *Reflections for Daily Prayer*.

Brown, William (ed.), *The Oxford Handbook of the Psalms* (Oxford: Oxford University Press, 2014). Forty-two chapters on different facets of the psalms, both ancient and modern, by a team of international scholars.

Gillingham, Susan, *Psalms through the Centuries, Volume One*, Blackwell Bible Commentaries, eds. J. A. Sawyer, J. Kovacs, C. Rowland and D. M. Gunn (Oxford: Blackwell Publishing, 2008). Paperback edition, with new Preface and minor revisions 2012. An introduction to the reception of the Psalter by Jews and Christians over two and a half thousand years.

Gillingham, Susan, *Psalms Through the Centuries: A Reception History Commentary on Psalms 1–72. Volume Two.* Blackwell Bible Commentaries, eds. J. A. Sawyer, J. Kovacs, C. Rowland and D. M. Gunn (Oxford: Wiley-Blackwell Publishing, 2018). A psalm-by-psalm commentary on the reception of the Psalter by Jews and Christians over two and a half thousand years.

Lewis, C. S., *Reflections on the Psalms* (Glasgow: Collins Fount Paperbacks, 1961). Discussion of key issues in the psalms from a Christian point of view.

Magonet, Jonathan, *A Rabbi Reads the Psalms* (London: SCM Press, 1994). Discussion of key issues in the psalms from a Jewish point of view.

The place of catechesis in the Anglo-Saxon missions

Marilyn Dunn, *The Christianization of the Anglo-Saxons c.597–c.700: discourses of life, death and afterlife* (London: Continuum, 2009).

Sarah Foot, *Monastic Life in Anglo-Saxon England c. 600–900* (Cambridge: Cambridge University Press 2006, paperback 2009).

Malcolm Lambert, *Christians and Pagans: the conversion of Britain from Alban to Bede* (New Haven and London: Yale University Press, 2010).

Henry Mayr-Harting, *The Coming of Christianity to Anglo-Saxon England*, 3rd edn (London: Batsford, 1991).

James C. Russell, *The Germanization of Early Medieval Christianity: a sociohistorical approach to religious transformation* (New York and Oxford: Oxford University Press, 1994).

Richard Shaw, *The Gregorian mission to Kent in Bede's Ecclesiastical history: methodology and sources* (London: Routledge, 2018).

Rooted in the Bible and history: How the creeds can help with faith formation

Barclay, William, *The Apostles' Creed for Everyman* (New York: Harper & Row, 1967).

Barth, Karl, *Dogmatics in Outline* (London: SCM Press, 1960).

Johnson, Luke Timothy, *The Creed: What Christians Believe and Why It Matters* (New York: Doubleday, 2003).

Kelly, J. N. D., *Early Christian Creeds*, 3rd edn (New York: Continuum, 2006).

Lewis, C. S., *Mere Christianity* (London: Collins, 2002).

McGrath, Alister, *Mere Discipleship: On Growing in Faith and Wisdom* (London: SPCK, 2018).

McGrath, Alister, *The Landscape of Faith: An Explorer's Guide to the Christian Creeds* (London: SPCK, 2018).

Williams, Rowan, *Tokens of Trust: An Introduction to Christian Belief* (Norwich: Canterbury Press, 2007).

Willis, David, *Clues to the Nicene Creed: A Brief Outline of the Faith* (Grand Rapids, MI: Eerdmans, 2005).

Wright, Tom, *Simply Christian* (London: SPCK, 2006).

Young, Frances, *The Making of the Creeds* (London: SCM, 2002).

Acknowledgements

Thanks to my fellow Pilgrim authors, Robert Atwell, Stephen Cottrell and Paula Gooder. Our work together and friendship has been a strong foundation for this project.

In Lent 2018, Ann and I hosted a series of seven gatherings over a meal in our home for around 120 clergy and lay people from every parish across the city of Oxford and most of the chaplaincies to reflect on what it might mean to renew catechesis across the city and across the Diocese. I was especially grateful to those who were courageous enough to admit that they needed help and those who were brave enough to tell me that I needed to do some fresh learning as well. Those conversations were hugely encouraging and inspiring and laid a foundation for the Study Days.

In September 2018, I made a pilgrimage of prayer across the city of Oxford over six days, travelling on foot and by boat, and prayed in and with every parish for the renewal of these ministries. Thanks to all those who offered such a warm welcome and came to pray.

Most of all warm thanks to Simon Jones, Carol Harrison, Susan Gillingham, Jennifer Strawbridge, Sarah Foot and Alister McGrath, the five Oxford theologians who generously took the time and trouble to contribute to a series of Bishop's Study Days in the Diocese of Oxford and to all six who have contributed chapters to the book (Jennifer was on sabbatical and not able to take part in the series). I've learned a great deal from the writings of each (some over many years) and intend to go on doing so. Thanks also to David Heywood and his team who co-ordinated the days and those who led workshops, and to the 450 clergy and lay ministers who took part.

Finally thanks and appreciation to my senior colleagues in Oxford who are a continual inspiration and to my outstanding support team: Marian Green, Sharon Appleton and Paul Cowan who supported each of these events (and so much else) with great patience, care and good humour.

My own part of this book is dedicated to the memory of Marian Croft, my mum, who died on the first day of the prayer pilgrimage and also to Caleb, our youngest grandson, who had the most difficult of beginnings but, thanks be to God, is a source of great joy.

+*Steven Oxford*
25 January 2019
The Feast of the Conversion of St Paul (and the courage of Ananias)

Index of Names and Subjects